SHARKS
of New England

Alessandro De Maddalena
with **Walter Heim**

This book is dedicated to

Antonio and Alessandra

ISBN 978-089272-813-8

Designed by Rich Eastman

BOOKS·MAGAZINE·ONLINE
www.downeast.com
Printed in China

5   4   3   2   1

Distributed to the trade by National Book Network

Library of Congress Cataloging-in-Publication Data
De Maddalena, Alessandro, 1970-
 Sharks of New England / Alessandro De Maddalena & Walter Heim.
    p. cm.
 Includes bibliographical references and index.
 ISBN 978-0-89272-813-8 (trade pbk.: alk. paper)
1. Sharks--New England. 2. Sharks--North Atlantic Ocean. I. Heim, Walter
(Walter D.) II. Title.
 QL638.9.D429 2010
 597.30974--dc22
                        2010020406

CONTENTS

FOREWORD

Sharks—big, small, fast, slow, dangerous, harmless—are among the most fascinating animals on earth. Disparate in their variety, habits, size, and shape, they inhabit virtually all the oceans, from limpid tropical lagoons to icy polar seas, but some are truly cosmopolitan in habitat, and can be found throughout the salty waters of the world. Very few species are restricted to the western North Atlantic, but there are many whose range includes the waters of New England across to western Europe. New England fishermen catch blue sharks, bull sharks, white sharks, threshers, and makos, but then so do anglers in California, Japan, and Australia. Some of the most notorious sharks (the "man-eaters") will be found in this book, but so will a number of small, harmless species that wouldn't (or couldn't) harm a swimmer if they tried. Here you will also encounter dogfish, catsharks, lanternsharks, kitefins, hammerheads, weasel sharks, and porbeagles. The study of sharks is a worldwide pursuit that can be conducted in the depths as well as the shallows, but New England, with its importance in ichthyological and popular literature, is an excellent place to start.

Richard Ellis
Research Associate at the American Museum of Natural History, New York
Author of *The Book of Sharks*
New York City
November 2009

A great white shark (*Carcharodon carcharias*) caught off Woods Hole, Massachusetts, in 1925.
(Paul Galtsoff / Northeast Fisheries Science Center, Woods Hole, Massachusetts)

Martha's Vineyard, Massachusetts, was the filming location for *Jaws*, the 1975 movie directed by Steven Spielberg.

(John Bortniak, NOAA Corps / courtesy of NOAA Photo Library)

PREFACE

New England was the location for one of Hollywood's greatest blockbusters, *Jaws*. The summer 1975 movie thriller directed by Steven Spielberg and based on a Peter Benchley novel. The fictitious Amity Island is the holiday retreat Martha's Vineyard, Massachusetts. When a gigantic great white shark begins to menace the small island community of Amity, a police chief, a marine biologist, and a fisherman set out to stop it. That's the story told in Spielberg's movie. Unfortunately, the reputation of sharks was considerably damaged by *Jaws*. The release of that movie contributed to people wanting to exterminate sharks. Sharks have much more cause to fear humans. Today sharks are decreasing in all oceans because of human activities.

The aim of this volume is to provide accurate scientific information on sharks that inhabit the waters of New England. New England consists of the states of Connecticut, Rhode Island, Massachusetts, New Hampshire, Maine, and Vermont. The latter is the only New England state with no coastline along the Atlantic Ocean. New England has a rich variety of 33 species of sharks, ranging in size from the 23.2-inch chain catshark (*Scyliorhinus retifer*) to the 32.2-foot basking shark (*Cetorhinus maximus*).

This book is primarily aimed at a broad and non-technical readership. The up-to-date and detailed scientific content, however, also makes it a useful tool for biologists. The book is fully illustrated by the first author, who has spent thirty years of his life depicting sharks. Beautiful photos that were mainly shot in the northwestern Atlantic Ocean by a number of professional photographers, researchers, and sport fishermen are also provided. We hope the reader will find this book revealing and informative. The biologists will find a huge amount of additional information in two classic textbooks: *Fishes of the Western North Atlantic. Part One: Lancelets, Ciclostomes, Sharks* and *Fishes of the Gulf of Maine*, both by Henry B. Bigelow and William C. Schroeder.

Alessandro De Maddalena and Walter Heim
Milan, Italy, and San Diego, California

BIOLOGY AND ECOLOGY OF SHARKS

Kingdom:	*Animalila*
Phylum:	*Chordata*
Subphylum:	*Vertebrata*
Class:	*Chondrichthyes*
Subclass:	*Elasmobranchii*
Superorder:	*Selachimorpha*

Along with rays and chimaeras, sharks are cartilaginous fishes, or *Chondrichthyes*. Their skeletons are composed entirely of cartilage, a light, flexible tissue that is even present in humans—in our noses and ears, for example. In fact, the only bony tissues present in sharks are their teeth and scales. The other class of fish is *Osteichthyes*, or bony fish or teleosts. Unlike sharks and their relatives, these fish have skeletons made of bone.

Sharks can be further divided into eight orders:

Hexanchiformes (frilled and cow sharks)

Squaliformes (dogfish sharks)

Pristiophoriformes (saw sharks)

Squatiniformes (angelsharks)

Heterodontiformes (bullhead sharks)

Orectolobiformes (carpet sharks)

Lamniformes (mackerel sharks)

Carcharhiniformes (ground sharks)

Within these eight orders are 31 families that include 479 species of sharks. This complex system of classification is continuously changing due to the discovery of unknown species and the ongoing study of shark morphology and genetics.

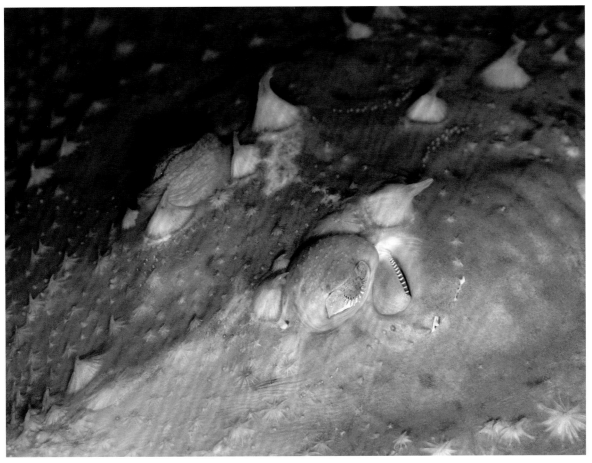

A thorny skate (*Amblyraja radiata*). Rays, together with sharks and chimaeras, are called *Chondrichthyes*, or cartilaginous fishes.

(Sarah Taylor / New England Aquarium, Boston, Massachusetts)

B ased on the fossil record, sharks appeared more than 400 million years ago, between the Silurian and Early Devonian periods. They most likely evolved from the placoderms, a group of extinct armored bony fishes. Shark fossils are abundant and have been found throughout the world. Complete skeletons have rarely been preserved because the cartilage rapidly disintegrated after death. Shark vertebrae have occasionally been preserved as fossils due to their partial calcification. Shark teeth, however, fossilize easily because they are highly calcified. Fossil teeth are very common, and are often the only remains of extinct species.

Sharks are considered to be highly evolved. They have not changed much over the last 100 million years, suggesting that they rapidly developed characteristics that made them very well adapted to their environment.

A fossil tooth of the extinct megatooth shark (*Carcharodon megalodon*) preserved at the Perkins Geology Museum of the University of Vermont in Burlington, Vermont, with cat. no. 10230.

(Perkins Geology Museum of the University of Vermont in Burlington, Vermont)

A reconstructed set of jaws of the extinct megatooth shark prepared for the traveling exhibition *Savage Ancient Seas*, hosted by the Berkshire Museum in Pittsfield, Massachusetts, in 2007.
(Triebold Paleontology, Inc., Colorado / Embedded Exhibitions, LLC, Colorado)

Although it is commonly believed that sharks are large, the majority are, in fact, rather small. Most are less than 59 inches in total length—measured from the tip of the snout to the tip of the tail. Female sharks tend to grow somewhat larger than males.

The smallest shark found off the New England coast is the chain catshark (*Scyliorhinus retifer*). At hatching, the chain catshark measures 3.9 to 4.3 inches in length, and the largest recorded size is 23.2 inches. The largest shark found in the region is the basking shark (*Cetorhinus maximus*), which can grow as large as 39.4 feet. The basking shark filter-feeds on plankton and is the second largest living fish. Only the whale shark (*Rhincodon typus*), which can reach 65.6 feet, is larger, but whale sharks are not found off New England. The largest predatory species (one that catches, kills, and eats large prey) is the great white shark (*Carcharodon carcharias*). It has been recorded at lengths of at least 21.7 feet, but it may exceed 26.3 feet.

In New England waters there are fifteen very large shark species confirmed to exceed 9.8 feet in length. After the basking shark, they are (maximum recorded size is enclosed in parentheses)

tiger shark (*Galeocerdo cuvier*) **(24.3 feet)**

great white shark (*Carcharodon carcharias*) **(21.9 feet)**

Greenland shark (*Somniosus microcephalus*) **(21.0 feet)**

common thresher shark (*Alopias vulpinus*) **(20.9 feet)**

shortfin mako shark (*Isurus oxyrinchus*) **(14.6 feet)**

dusky shark (*Carcharhinus obscurus*) **(13.1 feet)**

oceanic whitetip shark (*Carcharhinus longimanus*) **(13.0 feet)**

blue shark (*Prionace glauca*) **(12.7 feet)**

sand tiger shark (*Carcharias taurus*) **(12.5 feet)**

smooth hammerhead (*Sphyrna zygaena*) **(12.1 feet)**

porbeagle (*Lamna nasus*) **(11.8 feet)**

bull shark (*Carcharhinus leucas*) **(11.2 feet)**

silky shark (*Carcharhinus falciformis*) **(10.8 feet)**

bramble shark (*Echinorhinus brucus*) **(10.2 feet)**

nurse shark (*Ginglymostoma cirratum*) **(10.0 feet)**

A replica cast made from a 15.9-foot TL (total length) male great white shark caught east of Block Island, Connecticut, on August 5, 1983. The replica is on exhibit at the Department of Marine Sciences of the University of Connecticut in Groton, Connecticut.

(J. Evan Ward / Department of Marine Sciences of the University of Connecticut, Groton, Connecticut)

Body shape, or morphology, varies considerably among shark species. In general, most sharks have a streamlined body, a long flattened snout, a ventral parabolic mouth, and an asymmetric caudal (tail) fin, with a significantly larger upper lobe and a shorter lower lobe. There is some variation in this general body shape, however, due to habitat and way of life. For example, the benthic (bottom-dwelling) chain catshark is long and slender, whereas the pelagic (open-ocean-dwelling), fast-swimming shortfin mako (*Isurus oxyrinchus*) has a highly spindle-shaped body. The benthic sand devil (*Squatina dumeril*) has a compressed, flattened body.

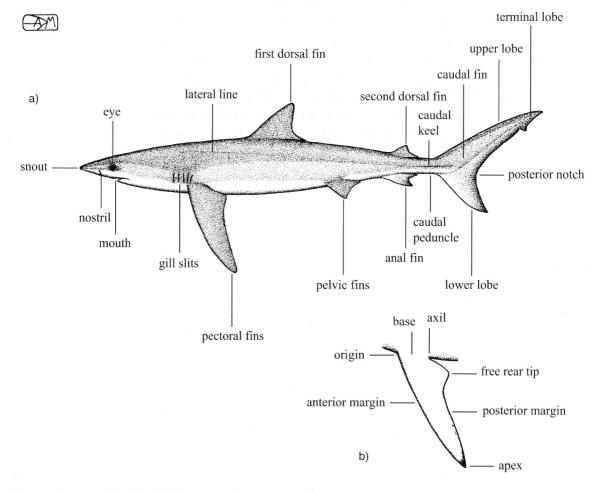

The external anatomy of the blue shark (*Prionace glauca*) a); parts of the fin b).

A shark's fins are fundamental to swimming, including propulsion, stability, and steering. Most sharks have eight fins, including a pair of pectorals, a pair of pelvic fins, a first dorsal, second dorsal, anal, and caudal fin. In some sharks, a fin is missing or reduced. For example, dogfish sharks, such as the piked dogfish (*Squalus acanthias*), lack the anal fin. The caudal fin, or tail, moves side to side and is used to propel the shark forward. The shark's flattened head and nearly horizontal, wide pectoral fins provide lift, which offsets the downward force generated by the upper lobe of the caudal fin. The shape of the tail varies from species to species. Some fast-swimming species, like the porbeagle shark (*Lamna nasus*), have upper and lower lobes nearly equal in size. An extreme case of asymmetrical caudal fin lobes is found in the common thresher shark, where the upper lobe is nearly as long as the body. The thresher shark uses its tail to stun small food fish. Besides maintaining stable swimming motion, the fins also steer the shark along its intended path. The blue shark (*Prionace glauca*) has large pectoral fins and a long, flexible body, making it extremely maneuverable. Some sharks have lateral keels, also called caudal keels, on the sides of their caudal peduncle that are flattened and expanded, improving the hydrodynamic design of fast-swimming sharks. Usually there is one pair of caudal keels, but the porbeagle has two pairs. The second pair is much smaller and located on the sides of the caudal fin, immediately below the peduncle. The fastest shark may be the shortfin mako, with recorded speeds of 21.8-35.0 miles per hour. Most of the time, however, sharks cruise slowly; even the fastest have relatively low average speeds.

The first dorsal fin of the great white shark has a stabilizing function. This specimen was photographed in a shallow embayment off Woods Hole, Massachusetts. (Ed Lyman / Massachusetts Division of Marine Fisheries)

Some sharks, such as the piked dogfish, have a spine in front of the dorsal fins and can use these dorsal fin spines as a defense against predators. This spine has also been useful in determining the age of some species.

In order to conserve energy, many fish have a mechanism to maintain neutral buoyancy. In most bony fishes, buoyancy is achieved with a gas bladder, a gas-filled sac in the upper part of the body cavity that offsets the weight of denser tissues such as bone. Sharks do not have a gas bladder, but they do have huge livers filled with oil that is less dense than water. This, coupled with their lighter cartilaginous skeletons, makes them only slightly heavier than sea water. Certain species have developed additional ways of increasing their buoyancy. For example, the blue shark has a low-density jelly in its snout. The difference in the overall density of various sharks is also related to their habitat. In general, pelagic species are less dense than benthic species, but still must swim continuously to keep from sinking to the ocean floor. Benthic sharks often lie on the sea bottom for long periods. Typical examples include the sand devil, which lies buried in the sand for a long time, waiting to ambush prey, and the chain catshark.

Many sharks, particularly those that are benthic, like the nurse shark (*Ginglymostoma cirratum*), lie on the sea bottom for long periods at a time. (Sarah Taylor / New England Aquarium, Boston, Massachusetts)

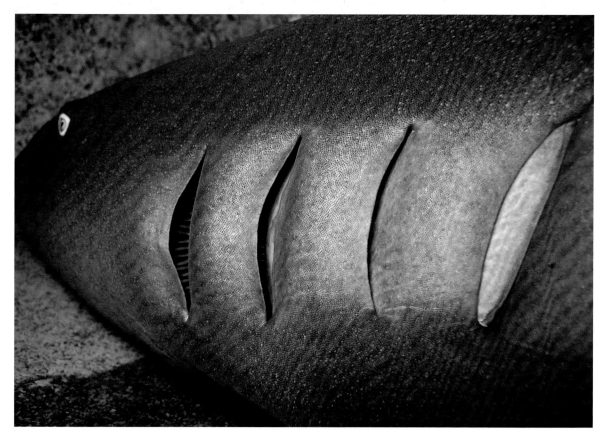

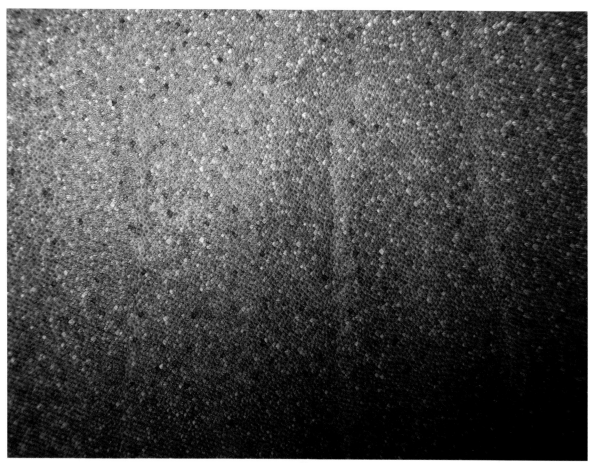

Close-up view of the dermal denticles or placoid scales of a nurse shark.
(Sarah Taylor / New England Aquarium, Boston, Massachusetts)

Shark skin has specifically evolved to increase hydrodynamic efficiency. The skin is directionally rough and abrasive because it is covered by very small to moderately large toothlike structures called "dermal denticles" or "placoid scales." These denticles are actually modified teeth rather than true scales. A denticle is composed of a pulp, dentine, and enamel-like vitrodentine over a bony basal plate or root that is set into the skin. They are configured to create small grooves that are thought to reduce drag. The shape of dermal denticles varies from species to species and from body part to body part. Their shape is also important in the identification of a species, especially when it is not possible to examine the whole specimen, such as in fish markets, where sharks are often cut into pieces.

The mouth size, tooth shape, and jaw morphology of each shark species are well adapted to the available prey. Most sharks have a ventral (located on the undersurface) mouth, though an exception is the Atlantic angel shark or sand devil, which has a terminal (located at the front) mouth. The mouth varies widely in size, from small to very large, and in shape, from parabolic to almost straight. Usually there are upper and lower furrows at the corners of the mouth that can be very short to very long (in the smooth-hounds their length is useful to help with species identification). Jaws vary considerably in size. Some sharks have spectacularly wide jaws, the basking shark and the great white for example. The thresher shark (*Alopias vulpinus*) has a small mouth and small teeth, which are suited for consuming small baitfish prey.

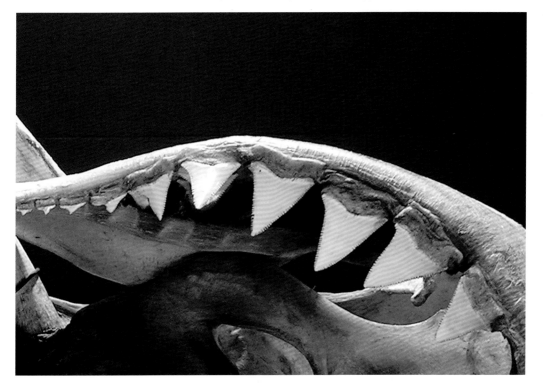

Upper jaw from a great white shark that was captured off Provincetown, Massachusetts, preserved at the Academy of Natural Sciences in Philadelphia, Pennsylvania, with cat. no. ANSP 69984.

(Academy of Natural Sciences, Philadelphia, Pennsylvania)

Modern shark jaws seem to have been derived from a modification of the first gill arch. In the cladodonts, the most primitive sharks, the mouth was terminal rather than ventral. Cladodont jaws were long, with the upper jaw fixed tightly to the chondrocranium (braincase). This kind of jaw suspension is called amphistylic and allowed little independent movement. In contrast, most modern sharks have hyostylic jaw suspension. Their jaws are shorter and allow the upper jaw to be loosely suspended from the chondrocranium, making the upper jaw highly mobile and enabling the shark to protrude the jaws.

The ventral position of the mouth does not restrict the ability of the shark to feed. As the snout rotates up, the upper jaw protrudes forward, positioning the mouth in an almost terminal position. Perhaps the best example can be seen in the great white shark. Its bite action is comprised of a sequence of jaw and snout movements. The snout lifts upward, followed by the lower jaw dropping downward. The upper jaw then protrudes forward. As the mouth closes, the lower jaw rotates upward followed by the dropping of the snout. The great white shark removes large chunks of prey by biting and shaking its head laterally (large specimens can easily remove 44 lbs of flesh in a single bite).

Like the dermal denticles, shark teeth are composed of a pulp, dentine, and enamel-like vitrodentine over a bony base. Each tooth is divided into two parts, the root and the crown. The projection of the crown is called the cusp. Many species have teeth with a large main cusp flanked by one or more auxiliary cusplets. Unlike most animals, the tooth of a shark is not fixed into a socket, but is implanted in the connective tissue of the jaw, known as the tooth bed. The teeth of sharks are often broken and easily detached, but they have a perfect mechanism of regular tooth replacement. Teeth are formed in a groove along the inner jaw, and behind the front teeth there are several parallel rows of replacement teeth. There are from five to fifteen rows of teeth in each jaw, and throughout the shark's life the teeth are continuously replaced—each displaced by a new tooth.

Sometimes teeth are lost or broken during feeding. In whaler sharks each tooth is replaced every eight to fifteen days during the first year of life, but replacement slows in adults, and each tooth is probably replaced every month. Sand tiger sharks (*Carcharias taurus*) at the Mystic Aquarium in Mystic, Connecticut, were observed to lose one tooth approximately every two days. Species with relatively large teeth tend to have one and sometimes two rows of functional teeth. Sharks with small teeth usually have more than one functional row in the jaw.

The number of teeth on the outer rows of the upper and lower jaws are used to help identify species. A dental formula represents the number and configuration of teeth in a shark's mouth. For example, the great white shark has a simple dental formula—usually 13:13/11:11. This formula is read as follows: 13 teeth in the right side of the upper jaw, 13 teeth in the left side of the upper jaw / 11 teeth in the right side of the lower jaw, 11 teeth in the left side of the lower jaw. Moreover, the dental formula often incorporates variability. For example, a great white shark's formula has a variability 12–14:12–14/10–13:10–13.

Teeth exhibit a wide variety of shapes, which vary between species according to their diet. Because of this variability, teeth are an invaluable means of identification. Teeth can be divided into three groups based on shapes common to sharks with similar diets.

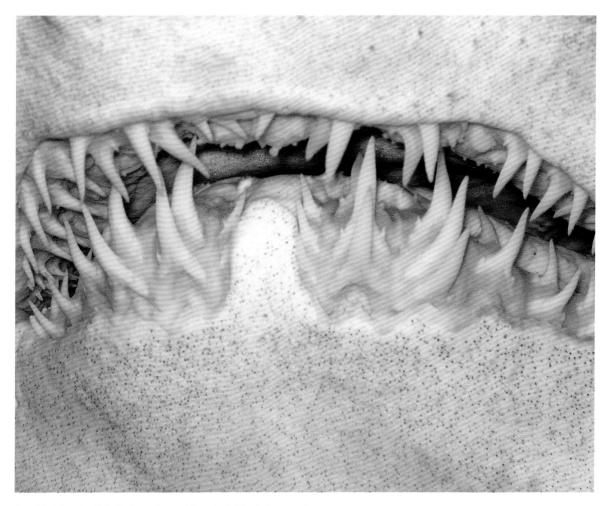

Functional front teeth in the jaws of a sand tiger shark (*Carcharias taurus*).
(Sarah Taylor / New England Aquarium, Boston, Massachusetts)

The first group of teeth are adapted for shearing or sawing pieces from large animals such as large fishes and marine mammals. These teeth are typically large, triangular in shape, sharp, and with or without serrated edges. The great white shark has this kind of teeth.

The second group are ideal for seizing smaller, faster moving prey such as small schooling fish. These teeth are narrow, with a curved shape, and tend to be moderate in size to very long. The shortfin mako and sand tiger have teeth with this shape.

The third group of teeth are used to crush hard prey such as molluscs and crustaceans. These teeth are smooth, with an almost completely flattened shape, and are arranged in a grid—like brick pavement. The dusky smoothhound (*Mustelis canis*) is among the species that have this kind of teeth.

Not all the teeth in a shark's mouth are the same. In most species, the teeth of the upper jaw are quite different in shape from those of the lower jaw—the teeth in the lower jaw are often smaller and narrower. Anterior (front) teeth are the largest and the teeth are gradually smaller working back, with the smallest teeth found at the corner of the jaws. As might be expected, teeth vary considerably in size from species to species. Some, like the great white and the shortfin mako, have spectacularly large teeth—the largest great white tooth measured 2.5 inches.

The shape of shark teeth is also related to the age of the shark. The tooth shape changes as the shark grows larger and its diet changes. In order for the shortfin mako to eat small, fast pelagic fishes, it is born with narrow teeth, but as it grows, these teeth become thick and strong to accommodate larger prey such as swordfish and dolphins. Young specimens of one shark species are sometimes mistaken for another species because of their tooth shape. For example, young porbeagle teeth are sometimes mistaken for those of shortfin makos because they lack cusplets, and young white sharks' teeth can be mistaken for those of salmon sharks (*Lamna ditropis*) because they have small cusplets and partially lack serrate edges.

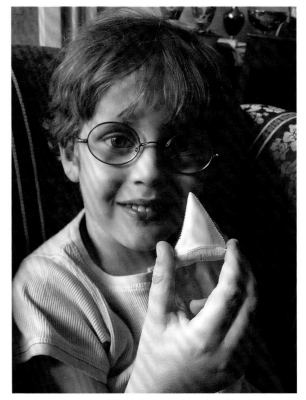

The author's son, Antonio, holding a tooth of a great white shark.

Respiration in all animals, including sharks, is the uptake of oxygen and the emission of carbon dioxide. Respiration takes place in the gills, which are the respiratory organ of sharks. While the gills of bony fish are covered by a flap called the operculum, shark gills are uncovered, making them external and clearly visible through the gill slits. While sharks have five to seven pairs of gill slits, all sharks found in New England waters have only five pairs of gill slits. A shark's mouth leads to the buccal cavity and to the pharynx, where gills are located. Water flows through the mouth, into the pharnyx, over the gills, and out the gill slits. As the water passes over the gills, oxygen is extracted from the water and carbon dioxide is released. This gas exchange occurs over membranes of the gill called gill lamellae, which have a high number of blood vessels. Some sharks have two small openings located behind or below the eyes, one per side, called spiracles. These are rudimentary gill openings that are used as an entrance for

This piked dogfish (*Squalus acanthias*) was caught by a commercial lobster vessel out of Portland, Maine. Note the spiracle, well evident behind the eye.
(Shelly Tallack)

water instead of the mouth. These openings are especially useful for species that live on the sea bottom, allowing them to remain motionless. Spiracles are larger in benthic species, such as the sand devil, which can partially bury itself in the sand. In contrast, spiracles are very small in pelagic species, such as the great white, or even totally absent in other species like the blue shark. Fast pelagic sharks, like the porbeagle, require a larger amount of oxygen, requiring them to constantly swim to stay alive. These sharks are ram ventilators, meaning their forward movement forces water through the mouth and over the gills.

Gill slits of a sand tiger shark.
(Sarah Taylor / New England Aquarium, Boston, Massachusetts)

S harks have a simple circulatory system, consisting of a single loop, with the heart pumping blood through the gills, through the rest of the body, and back to the heart. The heart is divided into two parts, the auricle and the ventricle. The blood is pumped from the ventricle to the ventral aorta. It then moves into the branchial arteries and then to smaller capillaries in the gills, where the oxygen-carbon dioxide exchange occurs. The oxygenated blood is then collected in the dorsal aorta and proceeds through the rest of the body via smaller arteries. After the oxygen and nutrients have been delivered to the organs and carbon dioxide transfered to the blood, the venous system returns the blood to the heart, primarily via the cardinal veins.

While most sharks have body temperatures equal to the surrounding seawater, some species of the order *Lamniformes* exhibit regional endothermy—they maintain a higher body temperature than the seawater because of a heat-retaining system. Off the coast of New England the species that exhibit endothermy are the shortfin mako,

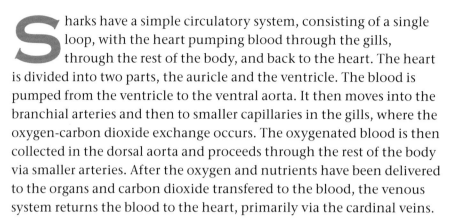

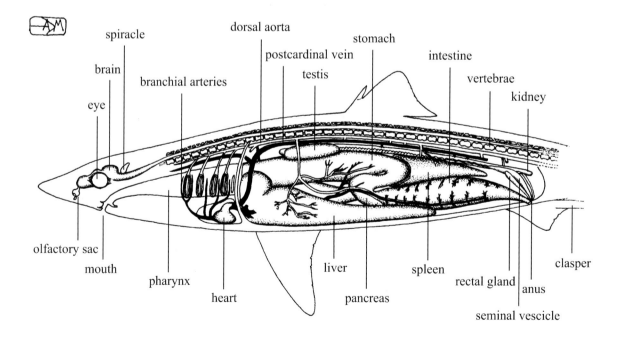

Internal anatomy of a piked dogfish.

A shortfin mako (*Isurus oxyrinchus*). This shark is a particularly powerful swimmer because it is among those few sharks able to maintain a higher body temperature than the seawater thanks to their physiological heat-retaining systems.

(Joe Romeiro)

great white, porbeagle, and the common thresher . For continuous swimming, red muscles are the most utilized. Endothermic sharks have large amounts of red muscle tissue located deep in the trunk next to the vertebral column. Nonendothermic sharks have these muscles more superficially located, such as just below the skin. Red muscle tissue is connected to the circulatory system by a complicated network of arteries and veins called the "rete mirabile," which functions as a heat exchanger. As heat is generated in the red muscles by swimming, it warms the blood that passes through venules into the rete mirabile. The heat is then transferred from the outgoing venules to parallel incoming arteries, so the heat is retained deep in the shark's body, rather than being dissipated to the environment. The higher body temperature increases the metabolism of these warmer blooded sharks. Having more energy at their disposal, they are very powerful, fast, and able to leap from the water. The high metabolism of these very active species requires a large amount of oxygen, so their gill slits are quite long.

Similar to most other vertebrates, digestion in sharks takes place in the buccal cavity, pharynx, esophagus, stomach, and intestine. In most sharks, the mouth, buccal cavity, pharynx, and esophagus are sufficiently wide to enable them to swallow large pieces of food. The stomach of a shark is very large, enabling these formidable predators to ingest whole animals, large chunks of prey, or a large quantity of smaller prey. Because sharks are able to ingest such large quantities of food at any one time, they don't need to feed often. Large, indigestible objects that are often consumed can be expelled, as sharks are able to evert their stomachs and regurgitate the contents.

The products of digestion are absorbed in the relatively short intestine. The intestine contains the intestinal valve—an internal structure that serves to increase the absorptive surface of the intestine without increasing the volume. This compact intestine provides sharks enough space for their large liver and stomach. There are three basic types of intestinal valves in sharks. The first is the spiral valve, which resembles an auger in shape. The second is the ring valve, which resembles a series of tightly packed plates with a hole through the center. The scroll valve is the third type, and resembles a loose roll of paper. For example, the piked dogfish has the spiral valve, the great white has a ring valve, and the smooth hammerhead (*Sphyrna zygaena*) has a scroll valve.

Studies have shown that shark digestion is slow compared to bony fishes. Initial digestion is relatively fast, taking around 24 hours, but it then usually takes 1.5 to 5 days for the food to be completely voided. The rate of digestion is species dependent, as it is closely related to the activity level and physiology.

A shark's stomach is very large, allowing a species such as the shortfin mako to ingest enormous prey whole or in large pieces.

(Joe Romeiro)

Sharks live fairly long lives—generally 12 to 27 years. But some species, such as the piked dogfish, can live at least 40 years and possibly up to 100 years. Sharks have a slow growth rate and consequently, depending on the species, it may take 2 to 20 years for a shark to reach sexual maturity.

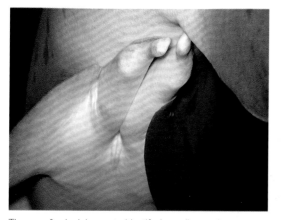 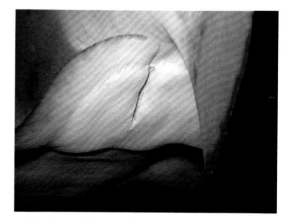

The sex of a shark is easy to identify depending on the presence or the absence of the claspers. The photos show the pelvic region of male (left) and female (right) sand tiger sharks. (Sarah Taylor / New England Aquarium, Boston, Massachusetts)

Fertilization in sharks is internal. Male sharks have two external organs called claspers, located at the base of the pelvic fins, that are used to impregnate females. In young sharks the claspers are short and soft, while in sexually mature adults they become calcified and long. The presence or absence of claspers makes it easy to determine the gender of a shark. In order to stimulate the female to copulate, the male bites the female both during courtship and copulation. Scars, called "love bites" or mating scars, can be seen on the body (flanks, gill region, belly, back, caudal peduncle, and fins) of female sharks. During mating, the male inserts one clasper into the female's cloaca (the opening that serves for both reproduction and waste elimination), where a groove in the clasper channels the seminal fluids.

Three different reproductive methods have been observed in sharks. The first is called oviparity: the female lays hard, rough egg cases containing embryos that are nourished by a yolk sac. The second method is aplacental viviparity: the female produces live young that are nourished in the uterus by a yolk sac. The third is placental viviparity: the female produces live young that are nourished in the uterus by a placenta attached to the uterine wall.

In oviparous species, the female lays horny egg cases containing embryos nourished by their yolk sac. In New England waters there are a few oviparous shark species, belonging to the family *Scyliorhinidae*. Egg cases of sharks are similar to those of rays. The photos show the egg cases of black roughscale catshark (*Apristurus melanoasper*) (left) and little skate (*Leucoraja erinacea*) (right). (Samuel Paco Iglésias [left], and Sarah Taylor / New England Aquarium, Boston, Massachusetts [right])

Aplacental viviparity is the most common reproductive method and most New England sharks exhibit this type of reproduction. In some of these sharks, two additional methods of nourishing the embryos have been observed, other than feeding from a yolk sac. Oophagy is the process where embryos in the uterus also feed on their mother's unfertilized eggs. Embryophagy, also called intrauterine cannibalism, is the process where embryos in the uterus will feed on their siblings. Shortfin mako embryos have been seen to exhibit oophagy and sand tiger embryos have exhibited embryophagy.

Gestation times in sharks are among the longest of any vertebrate. The average gestation period is 9 to 12 months, but can be 24 months in the piked dogfish, and is thought to be nearly 3 years in the basking shark. Litter sizes of sharks occurring in New England waters vary from as few as 1 to as many as 135 in the blue shark , but most species produce relatively small numbers of young, with litter sizes averaging fewer than 20.

Shark babies are called pups and they are born fully formed and self sufficient, able to live and catch prey without assistance from their mother. Many shark species segregate by gender and size. Nursery areas, often coastal waters, lagoons, or estuaries, where only newborns and juveniles live, have been observed for several species. For example, the New York Bight is an important nursery ground for great white sharks in the western North Atlantic. The existence of these areas reduces the risk of cannibalism. Moreover, here the pups are usually able to find a greater abundance of suitable prey. Many sharks may reproduce infrequently, such as the nurse shark (*Ginglymostoma cirratum*), which reproduces every other year.

Sharks have a highly developed nervous system and sense organs that are used to find prey. The senses are divided into four categories: chemoreception, mechanoreception, photoreception, and electroreception.

Chemoreception in sharks is through olfaction (smell) and taste. Olfaction is used to locate feeding areas. A pair of nostrils is located on the underside of the snout and lead to the olfactory bulb, where the olfactory sensors are located. Sharks have a keen sense of smell and can follow a faint scent trail to locate prey far away. For example, the slick produced by a large cetacean carcass attracts large sharks, such as blue sharks and white sharks, from more than a quarter mile away. Some species criss-cross the scent trail, while others swim upstream against the odor. As the shark gets close to the source of the scent and is stimulated by blood and food in the water, its behaviour becomes increasingly aggressive. Taste receptors enable the shark to discriminate food before it is ingested. Some sharks, like great whites, test palatability while the prey is lodged in their mouths. Taste receptors are located in the shark's mouth and pharynx.

The nostril is evident in this sand tiger shark. (Sarah Taylor / New England Aquarium, Boston, Massachusetts)

Some sharks have nasal flaps expanded as long barbels with chemo-receptors, and use these anatomical structures to locate prey buried in sand. These species cruise in circles close to the sea bottom searching for prey, their nasal barbels touching the sand. The nurse shark uses this predatory tactic, then uses suction to capture the prey.

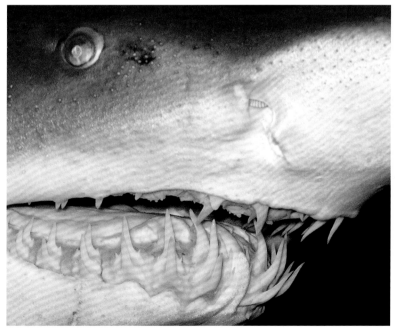

Nasal barbels of a nurse shark.
(Sarah Taylor / New England Aquarium, Boston, Massachusetts)

Mechanoreception in sharks is through the lateral line system, the ears, and the touch receptors. The lateral line system and the ears allow sharks to detect movement in the water. The lateral line is a row of sensory receptors located along the flanks and head. The receptors are pressure sensitive, enabling the shark to detect pressure waves from movement in the water. They are able to detect both direction and the intensity of movement in the water from great distances. A wounded creature, such as a speared fish, sends vibrations to the shark that indicate it is in trouble and therefore easy prey. These mechanoreceptors are also used to detect water currents. Sharks have a pair of inner ears, connected to the exterior by narrow canals called endolymphatic ducts. Hearing is related to the lateral line system, and is very sensitive to low-frequency vibrations, such as those produced by a struggling or wounded prey. Touch receptors are located all over the shark's body, and sharks obtain further information by bumping potential prey.

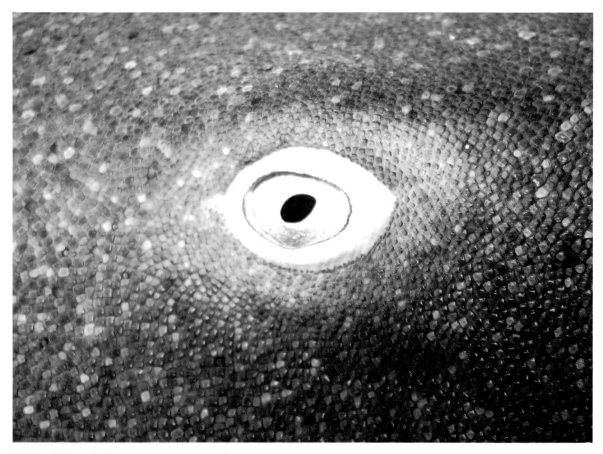

The eye of a nurse shark.
(Sarah Taylor / New England Aquarium, Boston, Massachusetts)

Photoreception in sharks is through vision, and sharks have excellent vision. Shark retinas are adapted for both bright and dim light, so sharks are able to see even in very low light conditions. The retina contains cone photoreceptors, which function in bright light, and rod photoreceptors, which function in dim light. The tapetum lucidum lies behind the retina and reflects incoming light back through the retina to restimulate photoreceptors, thus increasing the sensitivity of the eye. Some sharks have color vision.

Shark eyes have immovable eyelids, but many species have a third eyelid called the nictitating membrane, formed by an additional fold on the lower eyelid. This structure is movable and when the shark is feeding, the membrane closes over the eye for protection. Blue sharks have this nictitating membrane. The great white, however, lacks this membrane and in order to reduce the risk of injury; it rolls the eye backward during an attack on a prey.

Sharks use electroreception when they are very close to prey. They can detect the minute electrical currents generated by the nervous systems of prey by using electrical sensors called the ampullae of Lorenzini. The ampullae are numerous small sensory organs containing a sensory hair cell filled with an electrically conductive jelly. The external openings of these electroreceptors are small pores distributed over the head and are particularly abundant on the underside of the snout. These sophisticated sensors are very useful in finding prey buried under sand. For example, the smooth hammerhead uses its wide head, which has a great number of ampullae of Lorenzini on its ventral surface, to find and scoop hidden animals from the sand. Metals in contact with sea water produce mild electric currents, which tend to attract sharks. Sharks swimming close to a boat will often bite at metal structrures, such as the propeller, often ignoring baits. Sharks may also use ampullae of Lorenzini to orient themselves using the earth's magnetic field.

The external openings of the ampullae of Lorenzini on the head of a sand tiger shark.
(Sarah Taylor / New England Aquarium, Boston, Massachusetts)

Shark bodies are almost always dark on the dorsal surfaces (usually gray, brown, dark green, or blue) and white underneath. This color pattern renders them difficult to see by both their prey and their predators when viewed from above or below. When viewed from the side, some sharks transition from light to dark gradually, while others transition abruptly. This coloration is common in most pelagic sharks and is known as countershading. The fins often show a different coloration at their apex and posterior margin, and are usually dark, light, black, or white. Notably, the oceanic whitetip shark (*Carcharhinus lungimanus*) has white dorsal and pectoral fin tips, which are thought to attract potential prey within striking range as the spots look like individual food fish from a distance. Some species have a color pattern showing dark or light spots on the body, such as the Greenland shark (*Somniosius microcephalus*), the piked dogfish, and the sand tiger shark. A more complex color pattern is far less common, but can be found in the chain catshark, which has lines outlining saddles and sometimes forming a reticular network, and the tiger shark (*Galeocerdo cuvier*), which has faint bars on the side. Rare cases of albinism have been recorded in a few shark species. Among those that occur in New England are the basking and the great white shark.

The coloration of the chain catshark (*Scyliorhinus retifer*), reddish brown with black lines outlining dusky saddles and sometimes forming a reticular network, makes its identification immediate.
(Steve Ross, UNC-W, NOAA Office of Ocean Exploration / courtesy of NOAA Photo Library)

Most sharks favor tropical or temperate waters. Nevertheless, 33 shark species have been recorded to date in the New England area. In general, the farther north, the fewer number of shark species encountered. Only 17 species have been recorded in the cold waters of Maine.

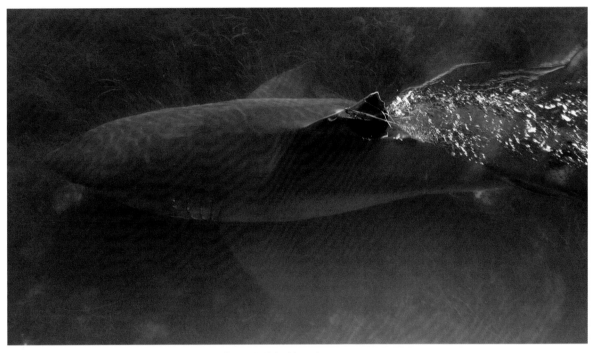

A 13.8-ft great white shark in a shallow embayment off Woods Hole, Massachusetts.
(Ed Lyman / Massachusetts Division of Marine Fisheries)

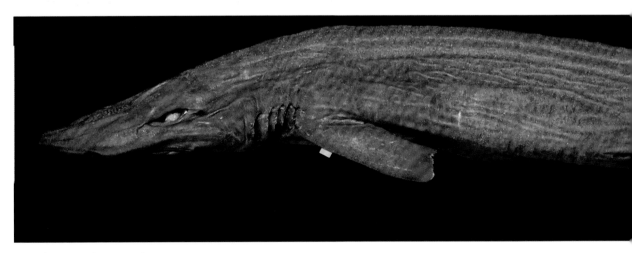

Sharks may be found in all the western North Atlantic and on any type of sea floor. Large sharks usually stay offshore, but some prefer the area close to shoals or the straits, where prey is more abundant. In very rare cases, large sharks venture into shallow waters, especially if the shoreline is located very close to a zone where the bottom becomes suddenly deeper. In September–October 2004, a 13.8-ft great white shark patrolled a shallow embayment off Woods Hole, Massachusetts, for at least two weeks. Massachusetts Marine Fisheries officials, using boats equipped with high-powered hoses, directed streams of water around the fish in an attempt to guide it to deeper water.

Most sharks spend a majority of their time on continental and insular shelves and upper slopes, typically at depths of fewer than 328 feet. Many of these New England shark predators, however, such as the piked dogfish, black dogfish (*Centroscyllium fabricii*), great lanternshark (*Etmopterus princeps*), Portuguese dogfish (*Centroscymnus coelolepis*), Greenland shark, kitefin shark (*Dalatias licha*), sand devil, great white shark, Iceland catshark (*Apristurus laurussoni*), ghost catshark (*Apristurus manis*), black roughscale catshark (*Apristurus melanoasper*), and the deepwater catshark (*Apristurus profundorum*), may visit deeper parts of the sea, going deeper than 3,280 feet.

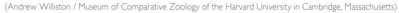

The black roughscale catshark reaches depths of 4,987 ft. The photo shows a 2.3-ft male black roughscale catshark caught in the Western North Atlantic and preserved at the Museum of Comparative Zoology of the Harvard University in Cambridge, Massachusetts, with cat. no. MCZ 125408.
(Andrew Williston / Museum of Comparative Zoology of the Harvard University in Cambridge, Massachusetts)

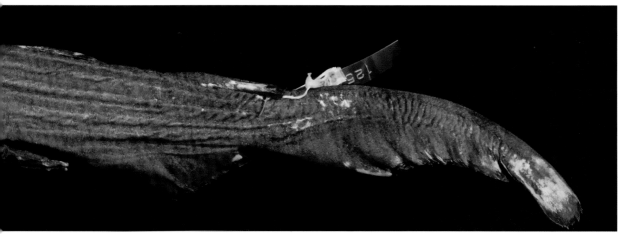

I n general, sharks consume a small amount of food, with the average meal being 3 to 5% of their body weight. They feed intensively for a short time and then will feed very little over a longer period of time. Most sharks feed at one- or two-day intervals, but can stop feeding for up to several weeks. During a period of nonfeeding, they live off oil reserves in their large liver. Researchers estimate that a 15.1-ft great white could survive one and a half months after a complete meal of fat-rich cetacean or pinniped. Food consumption is related to the activity level of a given species, hence the food consumption per day varies between species. Active species, such as the blue shark, consume more food than sedentary species, and some very active warmer blooded species, such as the shortfin mako, consume even more food.

Active species such as the blacktip shark (*Carcharhinus limbatus*) consume more food than sedentary species. (Alberto Gallucci)

Most sharks are nocturnal and actively feed after dark. Many sharks, however, are also opportunistic and daytime feeding by nocturnal species is often reported. Some species, such as the great white, hunt both at night and during the day. Certain species are vertical migrators on a daily cycle, that is they stay deep in the water during the day and ascend to the surface at night to feed.

Sharks usually inflict deep wounds on their prey. If the wounded prey escapes, it often dies later and may sometimes be found floating at the surface with the wide bite marks from the attack. Sometimes tooth-enamel fragments are found in the carcasses. Scars from shark bites are often found on tuna, swordfish, dolphins, and seals. These animals are often thought to have been hit by a boat, because the laceration patterns are similar to those caused by boat propellers. Bite scars and fresh wounds can sometimes be used to identify the species of shark responsible for predation and scavenging on various animals, although proper identification is usually difficult.

An adult male gray seal (*Halichoerus grypus*) that was fatally bitten by a great white shark at Chatham Light Beach, Massachusetts.
(IFAW Marine Mammal Rescue)

All sharks are carnivorous and many are able to feed on a wide variety of prey. Most sharks feed on live prey and some can track down healthy prey, while others typically feed on diseased, wounded, or dead animals. The size of the prey is related to the size of the shark, and most sharks generally prey on animals of comparable or smaller size. Among the prey species are bony fishes, cartilaginous fishes, molluscs, crustaceans, echinoderms, worms, pinnipeds, cetaceans, marine turtles, sea snakes, sea birds, and others. Even unlikely creatures like planktonic organisms, such as euphausiids, copepods, and jellyfish, have been found in shark stomachs.

Many sharks are opportunistic feeders and will consume a diversity of species depending on their availability in a given area. When one prey species is scarce, they feed on other species that are more common or easier to catch. There are also numerous sharks that show dietary preferences, and some species have a specialized diet. The common thresher is very specialized, feeding mainly on small prey such as anchovies, hakes, and mackerels. Great white and blue sharks seem to feed selectively on the energy-rich blubber layer when scavenging a whale carcass.

The dominant food source for sharks is other fish. Bony fishes are the preferred food and they supply a very important part of the shark's diet. The examination of shark stomachs has shown that, for most species, 70 to 80% of the diet consists of bony fish. Some sharks, however, seem to prefer cartilaginous fish to bony fish. For example, smooth hammerheads feed heavily on other sharks, rays, and stingrays.

Although fish are the primary prey of most sharks, some consume a high percentage of invertebrates, especially cephalopods and crustaceans. Crustaceans are the most important prey item of the dusky smoothhound, the black dogfish, and the bonnethead shark (*Sphyrna tiburo*). Cephalopods (octopus, squid, and cuttlefish) are the major component of the blue shark's diet. And in the nutrient-rich waters of New England, the giant basking shark lives on plankton.

The little skate (*Leucoraja erinacea*) is prey of the sandbar shark (*Carcharhinus plumbeus*). The photo shows an albino little skate at the New England Aquarium in Boston, Massachusetts.
(Sarah Taylor / New England Aquarium, Boston, Massachusetts)

Some shark species target marine mammals as their preferred prey. The great white and tiger shark will feed on both live and dead marine mammals, but most sharks only scavenge dead animals. Large whale carcasses are a common food source for species such as the oceanic whitetip and the blue shark. A few sharks, such as the great white, also eat marine turtles and sea birds, but at a lower percentage.

There is a relationship between the size of a shark and its diet. In fact, there is considerable variation in the diet of many sharks between birth and adulthood. Larger prey becomes increasingly important in the diet of growing sharks. Changes in diet are usually accompanied by changes in tooth shape. For example, the great white feeds on bony fish as a juvenile and begins preying on cartilaginous fish and marine mammals as an adult.

There can also be considerable variation in the diet of sharks from one location to another or within a season. Regional differences in diet are attributable to a higher availability of particular prey in that region. Thus, a migratory shark will feed on what is most abundant in that region. Alternately, a nonmigratory shark may feed on abundant migratory prey species that pass through seasonally. For example, blue sharks will gorge on squid during their seasonal migration to shallow water to spawn. In fact, many sharks focus their hunting activity on whatever species is currently most abundant.

A humpback whale (*Megaptera novaeangliae*) in the Gulf of Maine. Whales are commonly eaten by sharks after they die. A large cetacean carcass contains enough energy to sustain numerous large sharks for long periods.
(Captain Albert E. Theberge, NOAA Corps / courtesy of NOAA Photo Library)

Three species of sharks are responsible for most attacks on humans: the great white, the tiger, and the bull shark. The great white is responsible for the highest number of attacks. Although all three of these highly dangerous species occur in New England waters, they are uncommon or rare. Of all the other species recorded in the area, the shortfin mako, the blacktip (*Carcharhinus limbatus*), the oceanic whitetip, the dusky (*Carcharhinus obscurus*), and the blue shark have been known to become aggressive towards humans. Nevertheless, most of the sharks inhabiting New England waters are harmless to humans, but they should still be treated with caution and respect.

This close-up of a 13.8-ft great white shark was taken in a shallow embayment off Woods Hole, Massachusetts.

(Ed Lyman / Massachusetts Division of Marine Fisheries)

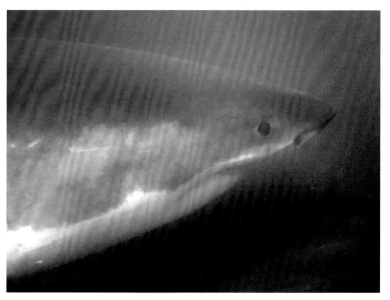

Pawtuxet Cove, Rhode Island. On June 23, 1955, a boy was attacked by a small sand tiger shark in these waters and survived.

(Russell Tayler / www.pawtuxetcove.com)

The Global Shark Attack File (GSAF) gathers data on shark attacks worldwide and is maintained by the Shark Research Institute (SRI) based in Princeton, New Jersey. The GSAF quantitative data is available to the medical profession, the scientific community, the media, and the general public in order to provide accurate and current data on shark and human interactions. In addition, the file gathers medical data in a format that can be utilized by physicians and surgeons called upon to treat victims of shark attacks.

Only twelve confirmed unprovoked shark attacks have been recorded in New England waters, and only three of them were fatal. The first recorded attack was in 1830 and the most recent was in 2001. Of the twelve unprovoked attacks, eleven were on humans and one was on a boat. To date, no unprovoked shark attacks have been reported or authenticated from either New Hampshire or Maine. Shark attacks are very rare incidents along the coasts of Massachusetts, Connecticut, and Rhode Island. The number of deaths from any other form of water-related activity far surpasses those caused by shark attacks, clearly indicating that human beings are not a part of the diet of any shark. Of the twelve recorded attacks, only four can be attributed to a particular species. The sharks identified as responsible for these four attacks were a great white, a mako, a sand tiger, and a blue shark.

The great white shark often attacks suddenly and without warning.
(Vittorio Gabriotti)

Areas of human activity in the water usually do not overlap the feeding areas of large predatory sharks. However, large, dangerous sharks do occasionally come close to shore, more often in zones where the bottom drops off very rapidly and prey are abundant. Islands, straits, channels, shoals, and river mouths are possible attack sites.

The great white shark attacks suddenly and without warning, charging its prey and inflicting a stunning bite. The victim typically never sees the white shark until it is too late. These predators have been reported to attack seals, sea lions, sea otters, dolphins, tuna, and humans using this method. This charge-and-bite behavior enables the white shark to disable prey with minimal risk of injury and minimal energy expenditure. The great white shark's approach to a prey can be horizontal or vertical and its heavy mass combined with the sudden impact disorients and stuns the prey. The initial attack is often followed by a short waiting period, in which the prey does not usually attempt to flee because of the initial wound and the onset of shock. When the prey expires due to blood loss, the white shark returns to consume the dead animal. This behavior has been termed "bite-and-spit." A high percentage of white shark attacks on humans, however, do not conform to this behavior. Although the bite-and-spit behavior is effective, it is not the rule for all white shark attacks.

In human attacks, the shark usually takes a fast bite out of the victim and then swims away. It has been suggested that after biting, the shark realizes the human is a foreign object and not its usual prey, and it immediately releases the victim. Some researchers have suggested that by biting the victim, the shark is determining whether the victim is suitable as food. Besides feeding, unprovoked attacks can be attributed to other causes, such as defense and social behaviors.

Buzzards Bay, Massachusetts. On July 25, 1936, a boy was attacked by a great white shark in these waters and died. (Edgar Kleindinst, NMFS Woods Hole Laboratory / courtesy of NOAA Photo Library)

DATE	VICTIM	ACTIVITY	LOCATION	SPECIES	OUTCOME
26 Jul 1830	J.B.	Fishing	Swampscott, Essex County, MA	Unknown	Fatal
12 Aug 1881	J.L.	Swimming	Providence, RI	Unknown	Survived
9 Aug 1890	R.O.	Treading for clams	Bridgeport, CT	Unknown	Survived
11 Aug 1895	C.B.	Swimming	Noyes Beach, RI	Unknown	Fatal
13 Sep 1900	G.B.	Diving	Coddington Cove, RI	Unknown	Survived
21 Sep 1922	Boat	Fishing	Nahant, MA	Unknown	Survived
25 Jul 1936	J.T.	Swimming	Hollywood Beach, above Mattapoisett Harbor, Buzzards Bay, MA	Great white shark	Fatal
23 Jun 1955	W.C.	Unknown	Pawtuxet Cove, RI	Sand tiger shark	Survived
24 Aug 1960	C.T.	Free diving	Off Eames Monument, Bridgeport, CT	Unknown	Survived
04 Feb 1965	R.R.P.	Scuba diving	Granite Pier, Rockport, MA	Unknown	Survived
21 Jul 1996	J.O.	Swimming	Truro, MA	Blue shark	Survived
21 Jul 2001	Boat	Fishing	Chatham Island, MA	Mako shark	Survived

List of confirmed unprovoked shark attacks along the coast of Massachusetts, Connecticut, and Rhode Island. Regarding New Hampshire and Maine, no unprovoked shark attack has been reported or authenticated from either location to date.

(data source: Global Shark Attack File)

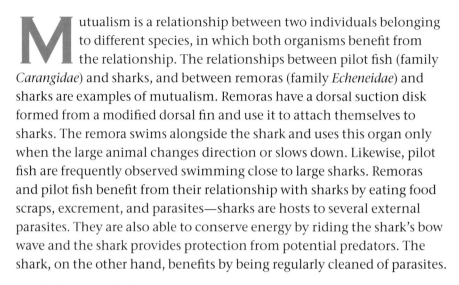

Mutualism is a relationship between two individuals belonging to different species, in which both organisms benefit from the relationship. The relationships between pilot fish (family *Carangidae*) and sharks, and between remoras (family *Echeneidae*) and sharks are examples of mutualism. Remoras have a dorsal suction disk formed from a modified dorsal fin and use it to attach themselves to sharks. The remora swims alongside the shark and uses this organ only when the large animal changes direction or slows down. Likewise, pilot fish are frequently observed swimming close to large sharks. Remoras and pilot fish benefit from their relationship with sharks by eating food scraps, excrement, and parasites—sharks are hosts to several external parasites. They are also able to conserve energy by riding the shark's bow wave and the shark provides protection from potential predators. The shark, on the other hand, benefits by being regularly cleaned of parasites.

A blacktip shark swims accompanied by two remoras (*Echeneis naucrates*). (Alberto Gallucci)

Two pilot fish (*Naucrates ductor*) swim close to a blue shark.. (Joe Romeiro)

Over the years, sharks have been deemed unpredictable killers of the sea. Only recently has shark behavior begun to be understood. Many behaviors have a communication function. These predators often attempt to communicate with animals, including man, using particular signals before executing an attack. These particular behaviors may function as a means of defending the shark itself, its pups, or its individual territory. Often the shark circles the prey or even bumps it before attacking. Sometimes even the great white and the shortfin mako show a threat display with a partial opening of the jaws, called gaping. The shortfin mako has been observed swimming rapidly in a figure eight pattern as a threat display. The correct interpretation of a shark's behavior, particularly the threat display, may avoid an attack.

A basking shark (*Cetorhinus maximus*) photographed off the coast of Massachusetts.
Basking sharks aggregate in the Gulf of Maine to feed from spring through autumn.
(Greg Sears / Mass Bay Guides)

Sometimes, when two great white sharks attempt to feed on a single carcass, one will raise its caudal fin above the water and slap the surface, splashing the water towards the other shark. This behavior has been interpreted as an agonistic display, where one shark is trying to force the competitor to flee in order to avoid a fight. Many sharks eat other shark species and some occasionally eat members of their own species. These social hierarchies may serve as an anti-predatory tactic in which the superior shark warns the subordinate shark. These hierarchies are often based on size, so smaller sharks maintain a distance from larger sharks. Social hierarchies between different species and among members of the same species have been reported. For example, great white sharks dominate blue sharks when both species are feeding on a whale carcass. It has been noted that blue sharks do not scavenge when the white sharks are feeding.

An oceanic whitetip shark (*Carcharhinus longimanus*) swims accompanied by some pilot fish. It has been suggested that the wide white spots at the apex of the fin serve to provide deceptive information to schooling fish and thereby attract them into the strike zone.
(Claudio Perotti)

A blue shark photographed off Rhode Island. Blue sharks show particular foraging behaviors when they find aggregated prey, such as a large school of squid. They simply swim through the aggregation with their jaws open, and fill their mouths with numerous squid.
(Robert Cantrell)

In studying the feeding behavior of sharks, it has been observed that these fishes have a wide variety of predatory strategies. Fast swimming sharks, such as the shortfin mako, swim faster than their prey in order to capture it. Others sharks take their prey violently by surprise, like the great white that charges up from deeper water. Some sharks, such as the sand devil, are ambushers, and lie motionless on the sea bottom waiting passing prey, then striking suddenly and very rapidly. Other species have developed particular strategies to feed on schooling prey. For example, the common thresher shark slashes the water with the incredibly long upper lobe of its caudal fin in order to herd and disorient the fish. The leading edge of the tail is used to stun the prey. Blue sharks also feed on schooled squid by simply swimming through the squid masses with their mouths wide open. Although many sharks use clever hunting strategies, no shark relies exclusively on a single tactic to capture its prey.

Most sharks are solitary, but they can also be found in pairs or in small to large groups. The piked dogfish is an example of a shark

Human beings are the only predators threatening the survival of sharks. Many shark species are of economic importance, and today shark numbers are decreasing in all oceans because of human activity.

Humans kill sharks for their meat, cartilage, skin, oil, and other products. Shark meat is consumed in nearly all countries, and in some nations shark meat makes up a significant part of the human diet. Shark meat is marketed fresh, chilled, frozen, smoked, and dried-salted. The species with the highest quality meat are the shortfin mako, porbeagle, and common thresher shark. The piked dogfish is also highly desired. The demand for shark meat has dramatically increased in the last ten to twenty years, possibly due to the recent dramatic reduction of commercially important bony fishes, which has caused fishermen to target sharks as a primary source of revenue.

Many sharks that are commercially fished are being overfished nearly all over the world. Among the species recorded in New England waters, the shortfin mako, porbeagle, piked dogfish, and the blue shark have been heavily exploited. In fact, the piked dogfish is the leading commercial shark taken in the world.

An estimated 50% of the worldwide shark catch is believed to be taken accidentally while fishing for other species such as tuna and swordfish. This unplanned capture of non-targeted marine animals is called "bycatch." Pelagic longlines are single-stranded fishing lines that extend for 11.2 to 44.7 miles and have an average of 1,500 hooks attached. This nondiscriminating gear is widely used in many parts of the world, including New England, to catch tuna and swordfish. In some areas, the number of sharks caught by longliners reaches 90% of total longline captures. Species such as the blue shark and shortfin mako are most impacted by longlining, but many others, such as the common thresher, are also taken. Shortfin mako and thresher sharks are usually retained for their market value, but blue sharks are usually discarded. Drift gillnets (entangling nets used to capture species like swordfish, sharks, and tuna) also take a heavy toll on shark populations.

Recreational fishing boats at Newport, Rhode Island. (Ben Mieremet, NOAA, OSD / courtesy of NOAA Photo Library)

Sharks are clearly more affected by commercial fishing than bony fish because of long sexual maturation times, long gestation periods, and small litter sizes. Moreover, many shark species, such as blue sharks, segregate by size and sex, so the exploitation of sharks in a nursery area can be particularly devastating. Shark populations are unable to withstand overexploitation as this has long–term implications for rebuilding the shark populations, which may take decades.

The commercial taking of sharks in the western North Atlantic in the past decades has certainly been much more extensive than it is today. Nobody knows exactly how many sharks are caught each year in the world, but the number is enormous. Annual landings of cartilaginous fish reported to the Food and Agriculture Organization of the United Nations (FAO) amount to around 820,000 tons, but the actual amount is probably much higher because large parts of the catch are unreported. Several thousand sharks boated by fishermen and released, either dead or alive, are not included in this total. Several shark species, such as the porbeagle, the shortfin mako, and the thresher, are also caught and kept by recreational anglers.

This piked dogfish was caught by a commercial lobster vessel out of Portland, Maine.
(Shelly Tallack)

Humans also have a less direct, yet just as harmful, effect on sharks. The depletion of the food resource by overfishing certainly affects the shark population. Other factors, such as environmental pollution, global warming, and habitat destruction are all contributors. Toxic chemicals that are absorbed or ingested by animals get passed up the food chain through feeding. Top predators, such as sharks, are at higher risk since several toxins accumulate in the lower levels of the food chain, and become concentrated at the top. Mercury, for example, is a toxic metal that has been shown to accumulate especially in the aged muscle tissue of predators. As a result, sharks, tuna, and swordfish can represent a significant unwanted source of mercury to humans. For this reason, fish markets regularly monitor the levels of mercury contamination in shark meat.

CONSERVATION

Because sharks are a fundamental element of most marine food chains, they play a vital ecological role in marine communities. As predators, they keep prey–fish populations healthy by weeding out the unfit, which contributes to the stability of marine ecosystems and maintains biodiversity. Shark predation is an important natural control on the size of many marine species populations. Being an apex predator, sharks have almost no natural enemies. Their eggs and young are susceptible to a very small number of predators, including some fishes and molluscs. Just a few creatures prey on adult sharks, such as other sharks and some bony fishes, like large groupers. In rare cases, some marine mammals, such as killer whales and sperm whales, have been known to prey on adult sharks. The decline of shark populations will likely unbalance the ecosystem and inevitably lead to increases in some prey species populations and declines in other prey species populations. The stability of marine ecosystems may be at risk.

Effective conservation and management of shark fisheries should be based on sound research in the biology and ecology of sharks, including the distribution, abundance, and exploitation. Understanding the biology and ecology of sharks can provide significant insights into protecting them from extinction. To better assess stock status and harvest impact, the life history of many shark species, including feeding behavior and predator-prey relationships, must be understood. It is also necessary to reduce the bycatch of sharks with better fisheries management.

Increasingly, professional commercial fishermen, sportboat captains, and recreational anglers are becoming more mindful of the plight facing many sharks. Instead of killing these magnificent creatures, they are tagging and releasing them for science, or simply releasing them. This is a practice I strongly encourage, and Walter Heim has actively tagged sharks for the past decade. In New England, Captain Greg Sears of Mass Bay Guides and his team, who operate on Stellwagen Bank and the shoals of Cape Cod, release most of the sharks they capture. But, they do harvest some sharks for biological study and consumption. The Mass Bay Guides team advocates the release of all sharks not intended for consumption and/or study.

A large blue shark hooked northeast of Stellwagen Bank, Massachusetts, in waters averaging 250 feet deep, by recreational anglers. Increasingly, professional commercial fishermen, sportboat captains, and recreational anglers are becoming more mindful of the plight facing sharks. Instead of killing these magnificent creatures, they are tagging and releasing them for science, or simply releasing them. The authors and the Mass Bay Guide teams strongly encourage this practice.
(Greg Sears / Mass Bay Guides)

Seven shark species found in New England waters are currently protected: the sand devil, basking shark, sand tiger shark, great white shark, silky shark (*Carcharhinus falciformes*), dusky shark, and sandbar shark. If captured, these species must be released. Only selected vessels participating in the shark research fishery are allowed to harvest sandbar sharks, and those are subject to the retention limits set forth by the National Marine Fisheries Service and may only be taken when a NMFS–approved observer is on board. At this time there is no commercial minimum size for Atlantic sharks and all legal sharks must have their fins naturally attached until offloaded.

None of the recent assessments by the National Marine Fisheries Service show any of the New England shark stocks increasing. The assessed stocks are stable or decreasing, with one exception. Piked dogfish were declared overfished by National Marine Fisheries Service on April 3, 1998, and added to the list of overfished stocks in the "Report on the Status of the Fisheries of the United States." Measures to end overfishing and rebuild the piked dogfish stock were immediately planned and this Fishery Management Plan was implemented in 2000. Eight years later, in the fall of 2008, data indicated that the stock was no longer overfished and was considered rebuilt. Consequently, the NMFS implemented a piked dogfish quota of 12 million pounds for 2009, and a possession limit (number of pounds per trip) of 3,000 pounds. This quota represents a 200% increase from the 4–million–pound quota from prior years. Although the yearly quota and possession limit have increased for 2009, piked dogfish remain a non-target fishery. Even with the increase in possession limit to 3,000 pounds, the market itself forces limits on the number of pounds of piked dogfish that processors will accept. Currently, all piked dogfish are exported as there is no U.S. market at this time.

A juvenile white shark caught in a fish trap, Woods Hole, Massachusetts, in 1961. The great white shark is now among the species protected in New England waters.
(Robert Brigham / Northeast Fisheries Science Center, Woods Hole, Massachusetts)

Many fishermen suggest that the piked dogfish abundance in New England has not only increased dramatically in recent years, but also that the populations have exploded. Captain Greg Sears of Mass Bay Guides has more than thirty years fishing in Massachusetts Bay. Until the commercial closure of piked dogfish, the ground fishing was excellent. Since the closure, dogfish populations have grown to a point that now they are so dense boaters are running them over, causing damage to propellers and shafts. The cod and bottom fishing has decreased to such a level that fishing regulations limit the catch of cod to five keepers per person on a full day trip. Captain Sears reports a decrease in all bottom fish species since the dogfish population exploded, and it is possible to catch hundreds of dogfish anywhere in Massachusetts Bay and still have the water around the boat swarming with them in a few minutes. In fact, he has seen the surface of the water covered with dogfish as far as the eye could see. According to Captain Sears, these fish are caught throughout the Gulf of Maine in excess by all types of gear because they are so abundant.

Sorting a big tow of piked dogfish.
(Fred Nichy / Northeast Fisheries Science Center, Woods Hole, Massachusetts)

Pile of piked dogfish on deck. Many fishermen suggest that piked dogfish populations in New England have increased dramatically in recent years.
(B.F. Figuerido / Northeast Fisheries Science Center, Woods Hole, Massachusetts)

Because sharks are difficult to study, there are many gaps in the existing knowledge concerning these creatures. Considering the wide distribution and large size of many sharks, the lack of data on many species has been scarce until a few years ago.

There are different ways to study the sharks in a geographic range. The first way is through studies that can be done on live sharks in their natural environment. This can provide useful data about shark behavior, distribution, and movements, especially through long–term studies and tagging programs.

The NOAA ship *Albatross IV* at Woods Hole, Massachusetts. The *Albatross IV* conducts fishery and living marine resource research in support of NOAA's National Marine Fisheries Service (NMFS), Northeast Fisheries Science Center's (NEFSC), Woods Hole Laboratory, in Woods Hole, Massachusetts.

(Commander John Bortniak, NOAA Corps / courtesy of NOAA Photo Library)

The Apex Predators Investigation (API) is located at the Rhode Island Laboratory of the National Marine Fisheries Service (NMFS), Northeast Fisheries Science Center (NEFSC) in Narragansett, Rhode Island. The charter of the API is to conduct life history studies of commercially and recreationally important shark species. This research is focused on distribution and migration patterns, age and growth, reproductive biology, and feeding behavior. API researchers conduct fishery–independent surveys of large and small coastal sharks along the Atlantic coast in U.S. waters from Florida to Delaware. Biological samples and catch data are collected at recreational fishing tournaments in the northeastern United States. API researchers also administer an extensive Cooperative Shark Tagging Program (CSTP) in the Atlantic Ocean, Gulf of Mexico, and Mediterranean Sea, utilizing thousands of volunteer anglers. The CSTP currently includes more than 6,500 volunteers distributed along the Atlantic and Gulf coasts of North America and Europe.

Tagging programs provide data on stock structure, distribution of species, including size and gender distribution, the exploitation of a resource by multinational fisheries, and migration. These programs have provided direct evidence of fish movements across national and international boundaries, including trans-Atlantic crossings. In addition, tagging studies can be designed with experimental components to estimate critical population parameters such as population size, recruitment, mortality, and survival rates.

A 2.8-ft sandbar shark caught in the western North Atlantic by the NOAA ship *Albatross IV*, which is preserved at the Museum of Comparative Zoology of the Harvard University in Cambridge, Massachusetts, with cat. no. MCZ 161213.
(Museum of Comparative Zoology of the Harvard University in Cambridge, Massachusetts)

The tagging methods used by the CSTP have essentially remained unchanged over the past thirty years. The two principle conventional tags in use are a fin tag (Jumbo Rototag) and a dart tag ("M" tag). The Rototag is a two-piece plastic tag (much like ear tags used on cattle) that is inserted through the first dorsal fin. These tags were primarily used by United States Fish and Wildlife Service (USFWS) biologists on small sharks during the first few years of the CSTP. As the program expanded to include thousands of volunteer fishermen, the dart tag was developed to be easily and safely applied to sharks in the water. The "M" tag was implemented in 1965 and is composed of a stainless–steel dart head, monofilament line, and a Plexiglas capsule containing a vinyl plastic legend with return instructions printed in English, Spanish, French, Japanese, and Norwegian. The "M" tag is planted using a tag stick—a forked needle mounted on the end of a pole. The dart head of the "M" tag is slotted so that it slides into the forked end of the needle tip. The tag is thrust into the dorsal musculature near the base of the first dorsal fin with the tag stick. Once planted, the needle tip is removed, leaving the dart tip in the musculature and the monofilament line and capsule protruding from the shark.

Numbered dart tags are sent to volunteer participants on NMFS self-addressed return post cards for recording tagging information (species, size, and sex of shark, date, location, and fishing gear used). In addition, first–time taggers are sent a tagging needle with instructions to construct a tag stick, tagging procedures, a copy of the *Anglers' Guide to Sharks of the Northeastern United States* by J.G. Casey, and a current *Shark Tagger* newsletter. This newsletter, an annual summary of the previous year's tagging and recapture data and biological studies on sharks, is sent to all participants in the CSTP. Tagging studies are primarily single-release events involving recoveries made by recreational and commercial fishermen. Upon tagging, sizes are recorded in fork length, total length and/or weight. Usually, these sizes are estimated at the time of tagging because the sharks are not boated, but in some cases the shark is actually measured. When a tagged shark is recaptured, information similar to that obtained at tagging is requested. Thirty years ago, a $1.00 reward was sent as an incentive for returning tags with the requested information and, after a few years, the reward was increased to $5.00. Since 1988, a hat with an embroidered logo of the tagging program has been used as the recapture reward. Throughout the program, special care has been taken with respect to identification of species. It was apparent in the first few years that fishermen had difficulty identifying sharks. Over the course of the program, there has been a continuing effort to provide shark identification materials to participants, many of whom have become experts in identifying sharks in their areas. The cadre of sport and commercial fishermen, scientists, fish dealers, and foreign fisheries observers send measurements, photographs, teeth, skin, and other materials to verify species identification.

API staff also manage and coordinate the Cooperative Atlantic States Pupping and Nursery (COASTSPAN) Survey, that uses researchers in major coastal Atlantic states to conduct a comprehensive standardized investigation of valuable shark nursery areas. Information gathered from API research programs provides baseline biological data for the management of large Atlantic sharks.

Bradley M. Wetherbee, of the University of Rhode Island Department of Biological Sciences, and his colleagues are studying long-term movements of pelagic sharks, taking advantage of the latest tagging technology. They have tagged shortfin mako and blue sharks with a variety of satellite archival tags. These tags have computer–controlled sensors programmed to sample and store depth, temperature, and geographical location data. Some satellite tags detach from the shark at a scheduled time and transmit all the data, while others remain on the shark and transmit stored data when the shark surfaces. The information is transmitted to the Argos data collection system aboard orbiting NOAA weather satellites. This information is then downloaded and provided to the research team for analysis.

This mounted basking shark was on exhibit to the public in the Main Hall of the New England Museum of Natural History (now named the Boston Museum of Science) in Boston, Massachusetts. (Museum of Science, Boston, Massachusetts)

Shelly Tallack of the Gulf of Maine Research Institute (GMRI) is studying piked dogfish. Tallack has addressed the issues of discard mortality and bycatch reduction of piked dogfish over the course of two separate studies. Both issues were founded on the concern that piked dogfish are frequently caught by all types of fishing gear targeting other fish in inshore waters during the summer and autumn months. Despite these high catch rates, dogfish landings have been heavily restricted in recent years in order to rebuild the stock. Tallack has worked in collaboration with commercial fishermen and other regional scientists to assess the survivability of piked dogfish caught by commercial hook gear (rod and reel, and longline). Another aspect of the research is the potential for an electropositive metal incorporated in the fishing gear to deter dogfish from biting. A 2007 field study tested the feasibility of incorporating slices of misch metal (an alloy of rare earth metals) into longline and rod-and-reel gear as a means of reducing the catch of dogfish on baited hooks. When catches with misch metal present were compared with those from control gear with no misch metal, the results showed no significant reductions in dogfish catch rates for either rod and reel or longline. Furthermore, video footage showed dogfish to have little regard for the misch metal as they persistently pursued the baited hooks. The study concluded that there is little evidence that misch metal significantly reduces catches of dogfish in the Gulf of Maine.

Shelly Tallack of the Gulf of Maine Research Institute (GMRI) is studying piked dogfish.
(Shelly Tallack)

A discard mortality caging study on piked dogfish was undertaken during 2006. In this study, commercially captured dogfish were transferred to cages and the mortality rate was monitored. The study took place in two locations, where Tallack worked in nearshore waters out of Portland (ME) and in nearshore Cape Cod waters by collaborators at the Cape Cod Commercial Hook Fishermen's Association (CCCHFA). In total, 2,418 dogfish were sampled. Mortality was highest in snubbed fish (23%). "Snubbing" is the process of removing the fish from the hook by force. GMRI observed significantly lower total mortality (7%) overall than CCCHFA (22%). In both locations, a gender affect was found, with males showing a mortality rate (26%) about twice that of females (14%). Larger dogfish were most resilient and showed the lowest mortality rate.

Another way to study sharks is by examining dead sharks captured in the commercial fishery. Information from the specimens is useful for a wide spectrum of studies, including external morphology, systematics, anatomy, diet, and reproduction. The type of data collected would include size measurements, gender, number of sharks caught, location, maturity stage, embryos, stomach contents, and parasites. Reliable capture data is available from fishermen via their logs or directly collected by on-board researchers. This knowledge helps researchers determine a species' geographical and bathymetric distribution, segregation by sex and size, and the existence of nursery areas. Besides being caught by commercial fishing operations, shark specimens are also caught during research cruises aboard scientific vessels. Even specimens caught by sportfishermen sometimes end up as objects of study.

Another precious source of specimens and data for the ichthyologists who study sharks are the museums present in the area. Museums in New England that own at least some shark items in their collections, include the Maine State Museum in Augusta, Maine, the Connecticut State Museum of Natural History in Storrs, Connecticut, the Bruce Museum in Greenwich, Connecticut, the Harvard Museum of Natural History in Cambridge, Massachusetts, the Peabody Museum of Natural History at Yale University in New Haven, Connecticut, the Berkshire Museum in Pittsfield, Massachusetts, and the Woods Hole Oceanographic Institution in Woods Hole, Massachusetts. Some museum specimens are accurate mounts of sharks taken locally over the years. Other specimens include entire sharks or parts of sharks preserved in formaldehyde or ethyl alcohol.

Sharks may also be studied in captivity. They are difficult to keep in captivity as they require large tanks and high water purity. In these unnatural conditions, they consume a very small amount of food, but can stop feeding for many weeks or months and eventually die. For these reasons and for other problems related to their physiological needs, many shark species are rarely kept in aquariums for great lengths of time, especially large or pelagic sharks. Captive specimens permit scientists to study swimming, sensory abilities, and, in some cases, reproduction. The study of shark behavior under captive conditions has been criticized because the behavior of a specimen forced to live in a tank is thought to be abnormal and not the same as, or even similar to, that of a free specimen.

Aquariums in New England include the Maritime Aquarium in Norwalk, Connecticut, Mystic Aquarium in Mystic, Connecticut, Gulf of Maine Aquarium in Portland, Maine, Maine Aquarium in Kennebunkport, Maine, New England Aquarium in Boston, Massachusetts, Maria Mitchell Association Aquarium in Nantucket, Massachusetts, and the Woods Hole Science Aquarium in Woods Hole, Massachusetts.

The Giant Ocean Tank of the New England Aquarium in Boston, Massachusetts, is 23 feet deep, 40 feet wide, and holds 200,000 gallons of salt water, with more than 600 animals, including sand tiger sharks. (Sarah Taylor / New England Aquarium, Boston, Massachusetts)

As the ecotourism industry blossoms, the general public is not only able to observe sharks in aquariums, but also in their natural environment. Scuba divers and snorkelers can join one of the many scuba diving trips organized around the world to observe sharks. One New England location where diving excursions with sharks are available is in Rhode Island. The owner of the Charter boat *Snappa*, Charlie Donilon of Wakefield, Rhode Island, has been in the charter diving business for 38 years. *Snappa* is a 46-ft fiberglass custom sportfisher outfitted for caged shark diving. Scuba divers must show proof of certification. The trips depart in the morning, meeting at the dock at 6:00 AM. The water temperature on site is usually between 60°F and 65°F in June and upwards of 70°F in September. Depending on conditions, visibility in the water may be as little as 15 feet or as much as 80 feet. The offshore water depth is approximately 200 feet on site. After a chum slick is started, it takes anywhere from 10 minutes to 4 hours for sharks to show. Divers must take turns as only three are allowed in the cage at the same time. The "anti shark cage" is cozy, having dimensions of 5 feet wide, 6.5 feet long, and 7.5 feet high. The cage is constructed from "sharkproof" anodized aluminum pipe and is positioned alongside the boat at a depth ranging from the surface down to 7 feet. Another observation platform, called "the Playpen," floats on the surface and is designed to allow non-certified snorkel divers to observe the sharks from above the surface. The blue shark is the most common shark that divers encounter, and the best time to view this shark is from July to October. Other species that are occasionally encountered include the shortfin mako and the basking shark. *Snappa* has also been involved with the National Marine Fisheries Service Cooperative Shark Tagging Program (CSTP) since 1976. Of the 1,958 sharks that have been tagged and released from *Snappa*, 203 have been recaptured—an impressive recapture rate of more than 10%. The most notable tag release was a 19.7-ft great white shark, the largest great white ever tagged for the CSTP.

This blue shark was photographed off Rhode Island during a shark cage
diving trip on Charlie Donilon's charter boat *Snappa*.
(Robert Cantrell)

Thirty-three species of shark have been reported in New England waters. These may be classified in 5 orders, 16 families, and 24 genera. The sharks presented here include very rare species, but do not include species without at least one confirmed record or those for which only anecdotal accounts exist.

Blue shark. (Joe Romeiro)

ORDER *SQUALIFORMES*

FAMILY *ECHINORHINIDAE*

Genus *Echinorhinus*

Echinorhinus brucus - Bramble shark

FAMILY *SQUALIDAE*

Genus *Squalus*

Squalus acanthias - Piked dogfish

FAMILY *ETMOPTERIDAE*

Genus *Centroscyllium*

Centroscyllium fabricii - Black dogfish

Genus *Etmopterus*

Etmopterus princeps - Great lanternshark

FAMILY *SOMNIOSIDAE*

Genus *Centroscymnus*

Centroscymnus coelolepis - Portuguese dogfish

Genus *Somniosus*

Somniosus microcephalus - Greenland shark

FAMILY *DALATIIDAE*

Genus *Dalatias*

Dalatias licha - Kitefin shark

ORDER *SQUATINIFORMES*

FAMILY *SQUATINIDAE*

Genus *Squatina*

Squatina dumeril - Sand devil

ORDER *ORECTOLOBIFORMES*

FAMILY *GINGLYMOSTOMATIDAE*

Genus *Ginglymostoma*

Ginglymostoma cirratum - Nurse shark

ORDER *LAMNIFORMES*

FAMILY *ODONTASPIDIDAE*

Genus *Carcharias*

Carcharias taurus - Sand tiger shark

FAMILY *ALOPIIDAE*

Genus *Alopias*

Alopias vulpinus – Common thresher shark

FAMILY *CETORHINIDAE*

Genus *Cetorhinus*

Cetorhinus maximus - Basking shark

FAMILY *LAMNIDAE*

Genus *Carcharodon*

Carcharodon carcharias - Great white shark

Genus *Isurus*

Isurus oxyrinchus - Shortfin mako

Genus *Lamna*

Lamna nasus - Porbeagle

ORDER *CARCHARHINIFORMES*

FAMILY *SCYLIORHINIDAE*

Genus *Apristurus*

Apristurus laurussoni - Iceland catshark

Apristurus manis - Ghost catshark

Apristurus melanoasper - Black roughscale catshark

Apristurus profundorum - Deepwater catshark

Genus *Scyliorhinus*

Scyliorhinus retifer - Chain catshark

FAMILY *TRIAKIDAE*

Genus *Mustelus*

Mustelus canis - Dusky smoothhound

FAMILY *HEMIGALEIDAE*

Genus *Paragaleus*

Paragaleus pectoralis - Atlantic weasel shark

FAMILY *CARCHARHINIDAE*

Genus *Carcharhinus*

Carcharhinus falciformis – Silky shark

Carcharhinus leucas – Bull shark

Carcharhinus limbatus - Blacktip shark

Carcharhinus longimanus - Oceanic whitetip shark

Carcharhinus obscurus – Dusky shark

Carcharhinus plumbeus - Sandbar shark

Genus *Galeocerdo*

Galeocerdo cuvier – Tiger shark

Genus *Prionace*

Prionace glauca - Blue shark

Genus *Rhizoprionodon*

Rhizoprionodon terraenovae – Atlantic sharpnose shark

FAMILY *SPHYRNIDAE*

Genus *Sphyrna*

Sphyrna tiburo - Bonnethead shark

Sphyrna zygaena - Smooth hammerhead

Some sharks inhabiting New England waters, such as the piked dogfish, the common thresher, and the basking shark, are very easy to identify even by a non-specialist. But identification is not as simple for other species. The morphology of a shark can often show high variability within a single species and juveniles may appear different than the adults.

Key characteristics to look for when trying to identify a shark are the size (remembering that it is possible to encounter a juvenile), body shape, length and shape of snout, absence or presence and size of spiracles, size and color of eyes, and the number, size, and position of gill slits. Teeth are excellent clues and can be prominent, with their shape clearly evident. For example, teeth are easily seen on shortfin makos and sand tigers. The shape and position of fins is possibly the most important characteristic in identification and, in some species, a dorsal or anal fin may be absent. Even color and color pattern can help in identification, especially when the shark shows a particular pattern. It should be noted that juveniles sometimes show differences in coloration from adults, particularly in tips and posterior margins of fins—they are often lighter or darker than in adults.

Dead sharks often lose the color they had while alive, however, careful measurements can be made on dead specimens and it may be possible to look closely at both the shape and the amount of teeth as additional tools of identification. If a camera is available, pictures should be taken, with some object of known length near the shark for reference.

Number, size, and position of gill slits are important diagnostic characteristics. This photo shows the gill slits of a sand tiger shark.
(Sarah Taylor / New England Aquarium, Boston, Massachusetts)

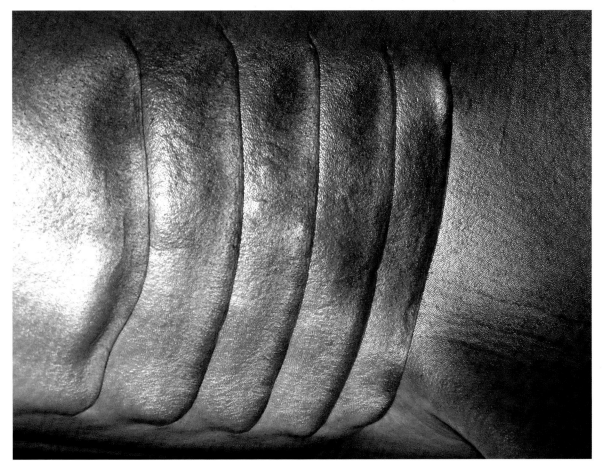

Bramble Shark

Echinorhinus brucus (Bonnaterre, 1788)

Order:	*Squaliformes*
Family:	*Echinorhinidae*
Genus:	*Echinorhinus*
Maximum size:	*10.2 ft*
Size at birth:	*1.0–3.0 ft*
Average size at maturity:	*Male: 4.9–5.7 ft*
	Female: 7.0–7.6 ft
Embryonic development:	*Aplacental viviparous*
Gestation:	*Unknown*
Litter size:	*15–24*
Maximum age:	*Unknown*
Distribution (area):	*Massachusetts*
Distribution (world):	*Atlantic, Pacific, and Indian Oceans*

Bramble shark: a) lateral view, b) ventral view of the head, c) ventral view of the pectoral fin, d) upper and lower teeth, e) placoid scale.

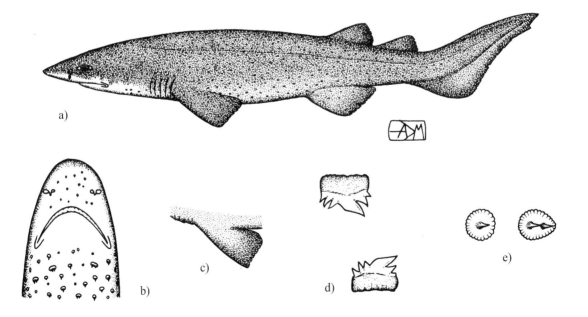

Morphology: Bramble sharks have massive and stout bodies with large caudal peduncles. The dorsal fins are located far back—the first dorsal is located over the pelvic fins—and both dorsals are nearly the same size. There is no anal fin. The pelvic fins are large and the pectoral fins are short. The upper lobe of the caudal fin is large and the lower lobe is short, and the caudal fin lacks a posterior notch. The back edges of the fins are frayed. Bramble sharks have very large dermal denticles (up to 1.0 in diameter) and they are widely spaced and pointed, with some fused in groups. The eyes are large, the nostrils are wide, and the spiracles are small. There are five pairs of relatively small gill slits, all located in front of the pectoral fin; the anterior (front) gill slits are shorter than the posterior (rear).

Coloration: Bramble sharks are gray-brown to purple-reddish on their dorsal (top) surfaces, sometimes with black spots. Their ventral surfaces are lighter or white. The dermal denticles are whitish.

Teeth shape: Both the upper and lower teeth are small, with a low, oblique cusp and two to four cusplets.

Dental formula: 10–2:10–12 / 11–14:11–14
(*Teeth in the right side of the upper jaw; teeth in the left side of the upper jaw / teeth in the right side of the lower jaw; teeth in the left side of the lower jaw*)

Diet: Small sharks, bony fish, crabs

Habitat: Benthic, mainly deep waters on continental and insular shelves and upper slopes, at depths ranging from 65.6 ft to at least 2,952.8 ft

Behavior: Sluggish, solitary, and timid

Threat to humans: Not dangerous

Notes: The only record for the region is an individual that drifted ashore at Provincetown, on Cape Cod, Massachusetts.

Piked or Spiny Dogfish

Squalus acanthias (Smith & Radcliffe, 1912)

Order:	*Squaliformes*
Family:	*Squalidae*
Genus:	*Squalus*
Maximum size:	*5.3 ft*
Size at birth:	*8.7–13.0 in*
Average size at maturity:	*Male: 1.8–2.6 ft*
	Female: 2.0–3.3 ft
Embryonic development:	*Aplacental viviparous*
Gestation:	*18–24 months*
Litter size:	*1–20*
Maximum age:	*At least 40 years, possibly up to 100 years*
Distribution (area):	*All New England*
Distribution (world):	*Atlantic and Pacific Oceans*

Piked dogfish: a) lateral view, b) ventral view of the head, c) ventral view of the pectoral fin, d) upper and lower teeth, e) placoid scale.

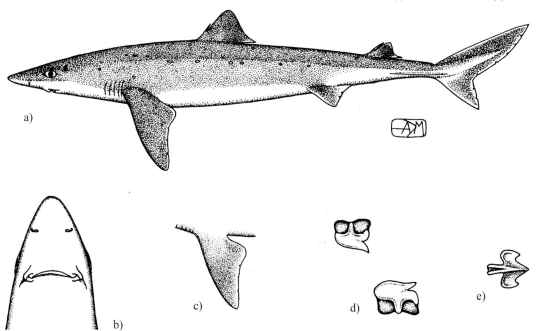

Morphology: Piked dogfish do not have an anal fin. Both dorsal fins have spines; the first dorsal fin is moderately large with a short spine, the second dorsal fin is smaller, but with a slightly longer spine than the first. The first dorsal fin begins behind the rear tip of the pectoral fin. The pectoral fins are moderately wide. The upper lobe of the caudal fin is moderately long, the lower lobe is short, and there are small caudal keels. Piked dogfish have a long snout and an almost straight mouth with long labial folds. The eyes and spiracles are large, and there are five pairs of short gill slits, all located ahead of the pectoral fin.

Coloration: The dorsal surfaces of piked dogfish are gray-bluish, or brown, with some small, white spots. The ventral surfaces are white. The pectoral, pelvic, and caudal fins have a light margin along the back edge, and the tip of the first dorsal fin is dark. The undersides of the pectoral fins are gray like the top surface, but faded toward the base of the fin and blending to white at the trailing edge. In adults, the white spots may be partially faded, sometimes disappearing altogether.

Teeth shape: Both the upper and lower teeth are similar—with one cusp, they are small, oblique, almost horizontal, and have cutting edges. The teeth are interlocked to form a sort of cutting wall.

Dental formula: 12–14 : 12–14 / 11–12 : 11–12

Diet: Bony and cartilaginous fishes, cephalopods, gastropods, crustaceans, polychaetes, sea cucumbers, ctenophores, hydrozoans, jellyfish.

Habitat: Pelagic, on continental and insular shelves and upper slopes, at depths ranging from the surface to at least 4,055 ft. Males can be found in shallower waters than females, though pregnant females can give birth in shallow water.

Behavior: Piked dogfish are active and can be found individually or in enormous groups. They are migratory and may segregate by sex and size. They are also rather timid and use their dorsal fin spines for defense.

Threat to humans: Not dangerous

Notes: Piked dogfish were declared overfished by the National Marine Fisheries Service in 1998, and added to the list of overfished stocks in the "Report on the Status of the Fisheries of the United States." Measures to end overfishing and rebuild the piked dogfish stock were developed. In the fall of 2008, data indicated that the stock was no longer in danger and could be considered rebuilt. This small shark is now extremely abundant in all New England waters, and fishermen report a decrease in all bottom fish species since the piked dogfish population has exploded, likely due to feeding by the healthy stocks.

Black Dogfish
Centroscyllium fabricii (Reinhardt, 1825)

Order:	*Squaliformes*
Family:	*Etmopteridae*
Genus:	*Centroscyllium*
Maximum size:	*2.8–3.5 ft*
Size at birth:	*5.5 in*
Average size at maturity:	*Male: 1.5–1.6 ft*
	Female: 1.6–2.2 ft
Embryonic development:	*Aplacental viviparous*
Gestation:	*Unknown*
Litter size:	*6–7*
Maximum age:	*Unknown*
Distribution (area):	*All New England*
Distribution (world):	*Atlantic Ocean*

Black dogfish: a) lateral view, b) ventral view of the head, c) ventral view of the pectoral fin, d) upper and lower teeth, e) placoid scale.

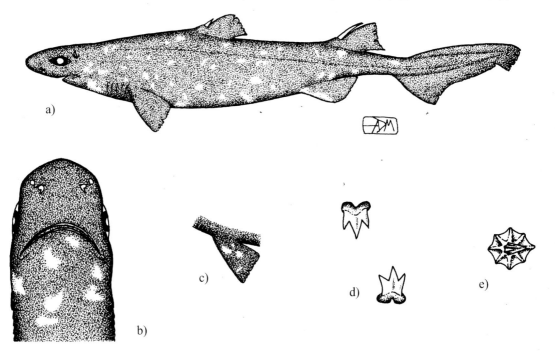

Morphology: As with the piked dogfish, black dogfish do not have an anal fin, and there are spines on both dorsal fins, the first spine is relatively short, the second spine is longer. The first dorsal fin is small and it is behind the rear tip of the pectoral fin. The second dorsal fin is slightly larger than the first. The pectoral fins are short and small, and the caudal fin has a very short lower lobe, a moderately long upper lobe, and a large terminal lobe. The snout is long and the mouth is sharply curved with long labial folds. The eyes and spiracles are large. There are five pairs of short gill slits, all located in front of the pectoral fins.

Coloration: Both the dorsal and ventral surfaces are brownish-black with irregular white patches.

Teeth shape: The upper and lower teeth are small, with one cusp and two slightly smaller cusplets.

Dental formula: 34:34 / 34:34

Diet: Crustaceans, cephalopods, jellyfish, bony fish, carcasses

Habitat: Pelagic, mainly in deep water on outer continental shelves and upper slopes at depths ranging from 590.5 ft to at least 5,249.3 ft

Behavior: Black dogfish occur in small to large groups. They are equipped with bioluminescent organs in the skin—possibly enabling these sharks to recognize others of their species, to coordinate schooling and mating behavior in the darkness of the deep sea, and to attract prey.

Threat to humans: Not dangerous

Notes: In the years when a long line fishery for halibut was thriving, black dogfish were often caught along the slopes of offshore banks, ranging from Grand Banks to Browns Bank and to the eastern part of Georges Bank. They were generally caught on sets at 1,197.5 ft or deeper.

(Andrey Dolgov / PINRO)

Great Lanternshark

Etmopterus princeps (Collett, 1904)

Order:	*Squaliformes*
Family:	*Etmopteridae*
Genus:	*Etmopterus*
Maximum size:	*29.5 in*
Size at birth:	*Unknown*
Average size at maturity:	*Male: 21.7 in*
	Female: Unknown
Embryonic development:	*Possibly aplacental viviparous*
Gestation:	*Unknown*
Litter size:	*Unknown*
Maximum age:	*Unknown*
Distribution (area):	*All New England*
Distribution (world):	*Atlantic and possibly Pacific Oceans*

Great lanternshark: a) lateral view, b) ventral view of the head, c) ventral view of the pectoral fin, d) upper and lower teeth, e) placoid scale.

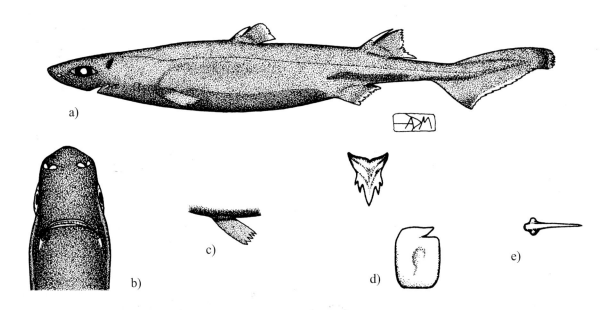

Morphology: Great lanternsharks have a slender body and generally small fins that are often frayed on their trailing edges. There is no anal fin. Both dorsal fins have spines—the first spine is relatively short, the second is longer. The first dorsal fin is small and begins behind the rear tip of the pectoral fin. The second dorsal is slightly larger. The pectoral fins are very small and the caudal fin has a short lower lobe and a moderately long upper lobe, with a large terminal lobe. The snout is long and the mouth is almost straight with relatively short labial folds. The eyes, nostrils, and spiracles are all large. There are five pairs of short gill slits, all located in front of the pectoral fin. Small photophores are located in the skin.

Coloration: Great lanternsharks are blackish in color all over their bodies. Sometimes the back edges of the dorsal fins are white.

Teeth shape: The upper teeth are very small, with one cusp and two to six cusplets. The lower teeth are larger, have one cusp, and are oblique, almost horizontal, with cutting edges. The teeth are interlocked to form a cutting wall.

Dental formula: 14–16 : 14–16 / 20–25 : 20–25

Diet: Unknown

Habitat: Benthic, in deep water on continental slopes at depths ranging from 1,860.2 ft to at least 8,202 ft

Behavior: Great lanternsharks have bioluminescent organs distributed in their skin, possibly enabling these sharks to recognize others of their species, to coordinate schooling and mating behavior in the dark, and to attract prey.

Threat to humans: Not dangerous

Notes: Great lanternsharks are common in New England waters.

(Andrey Dolgov / PINRO)

Portuguese Dogfish

Centroscymnus coelolepis (Bocage & Capello, 1864)

Order:	*Squaliformes*
Family:	*Somniosidae*
Genus:	*Centroscymnus*
Maximum size:	*4.0 ft*
Size at birth:	*7.5–11.8 in*
Average size at maturity:	*Male: 2.7 ft*
	Female: 3.2 ft
Embryonic development:	*Aplacental viviparous*
Gestation:	*Approx. 26 months*
Litter size:	*5–17*
Maximum age:	*Unknown*
Distribution (area):	*All New England*
Distribution (world):	*Atlantic and Pacific Oceans*

Portuguese dogfish: a) lateral view, b) ventral view of the head, c) ventral view of the pectoral fin, d) upper and lower teeth, e) placoid scale.

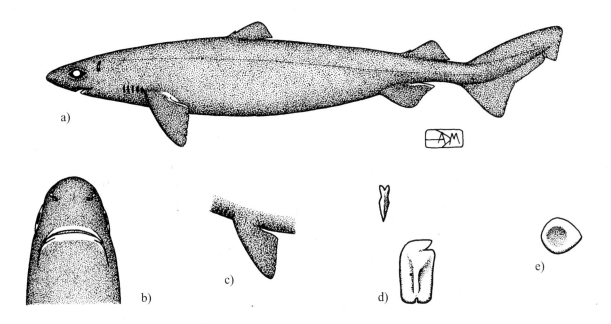

Morphology: As with other dogfish, Portuguese dogfish have spines on both dorsal fins, though they are very short. There is no anal fin, and the first dorsal fin is small and located behind the pectoral fin. The second dorsal fin is slightly larger than the first. The pectoral fins are short, and the caudal fin has a short lower lobe and moderately long upper lobe with a large terminal lobe. The lower labial folds at the mouth are long, and the eyes and spiracles are large. There are five pairs of short gill slits, all located in front of the pectoral fins.

Coloration: Both dorsal and ventral surfaces are a dark golden brown or blackish with metallic flecks.

Teeth shape: The upper teeth are small, narrow, and pointed, with one cusp. The lower teeth are larger, with one cusp, almost horizontal, and with cutting edges.

Dental formula: 29–35 : 29–35 / 19–21 : 19–21

Diet: Bony fish, sharks, crustaceans, cephalopods, gastropods, foraminifera, cetaceans, and carcasses.

Habitat: Mainly benthic, in deep water on continental slopes at depths ranging from 885.8 ft to at least 12,139.1 ft

Behavior: Portuguese dogfish are sluggish. They have been classified as facultative ectoparasites, since they obtain sustenance both from external parts of larger living organisms (taking bites out of live prey) and from whole smaller prey.

Threat to humans: Not dangerous

Notes: Portuguese dogfish appear to be uncommon in New England waters, but this is probably misleading due to the lack of a deepwater fishery.

(Pedro Miguel Niny Cambraia Duarte © ImagDOP)

Greenland Shark
Somniosus microcephalus (Bloch & Schneider, 1801)

Order:	*Squaliformes*
Family:	*Somniosidae*
Genus:	*Somniosus*
Maximum size:	*21.0–24.0 ft*
Size at birth:	*14.6 in*
Average size at maturity:	*Male: Unknown*
	Female: about 16.4 ft
Embryonic development:	*Aplacental viviparous*
Gestation:	*Unknown*
Litter size:	*10*
Maximum age:	*Unknown*
Distribution (area):	*All New England*
Distribution (world):	*Atlantic Ocean*

Greenland shark: a) lateral view, b) ventral view of the head, c) ventral view of the pectoral fin, d) upper and lower teeth, e) placoid scale.

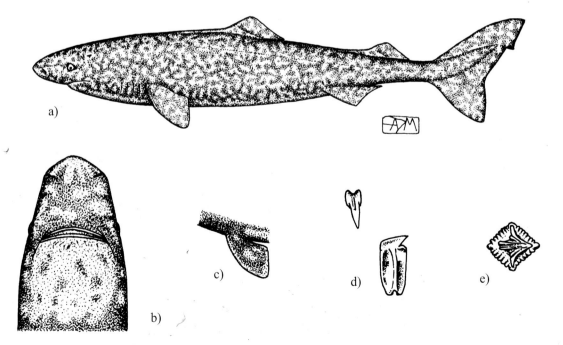

Morphology: Greenland sharks have a cylindrical body and lack an anal fin. The pectoral fins are short and the dorsals are low. The first dorsal is behind the rear tip of the pectoral fin and is slightly larger than the second dorsal fin. There is a low ridge in front of both dorsal fins. The upper lobe of the caudal fin is moderately long, with a large terminal lobe; the lower lobe is nearly as large as the upper. The snout is rounded and the mouth is almost straight, with long lower labial folds. The spiracles are small and there are five pairs of short gill slits, all located ahead of the pectoral fin and lower down on the body.

Coloration: Both dorsal and ventral surfaces are gray or brown, sometimes with numerous whitish spots.

Teeth shape: The upper teeth are small and vertical, with smooth edges, and have one cusp. The lower teeth are larger, with one cusp. They are oblique, nearly horizontal, and have cutting edges. The teeth interlock to form a cutting wall.

Dental formula: 22–26 : 22–26 / 24–26 : 24–26

Diet: Bony fish, marine mammals, molluscs, crustaceans, echinoderms, jellyfish, sea birds, carcasses.

Habitat: Pelagic, on continental and insular shelves and upper slopes at depths ranging from the surface to at least 3,937.0 ft.

Behavior: Sluggish, may approach divers closely (without showing any aggressive behavior). Greenland sharks are hosts to a copepod parasite (*Ommatokoita elongata*) that attaches itself to the cornea of the shark's eye. The relationship between these copepods and sharks may be a case of mutualism, since the whitish-yellow copepods may induce prey to approach close enough for the shark to capture them. In general, these infections do not significantly debilitate the shark, but in some cases vision is severely impaired.

Threat to humans: Not dangerous

Notes: Greenland sharks are uncommon in New England waters, though they might stray into the Gulf of Maine at any time of year. They may have been more numerous in the Gulf of Maine in early Colonial times, when Atlantic right whales (*Eubalaena glacialis*) were present in large numbers off the Massachusetts coast.

(Jeffrey Gallant)

Kitefin Shark
Dalatias licha (Bonnaterre, 1788)

Order:	*Squaliformes*
Family:	*Dalatiidae*
Genus:	*Dalatias*
Maximum size:	*6.0 ft*
Size at birth:	*11.8–14.6 in*
Average size at maturity:	*Male: 2.5–4.0 ft*
	Female: 3.8–5.2 ft
Embryonic development:	*Aplacental viviparous*
Gestation:	*Unknown*
Litter size:	*3–16*
Maximum age:	*Unknown*
Distribution (area):	*Georges Bank*
Distribution (world):	*Atlantic, Pacific and Indian Oceans*

Kitefin shark: a) lateral view, b) ventral view of the head, c) ventral view of the pectoral fin, d) upper and lower teeth, e) placoid scale.

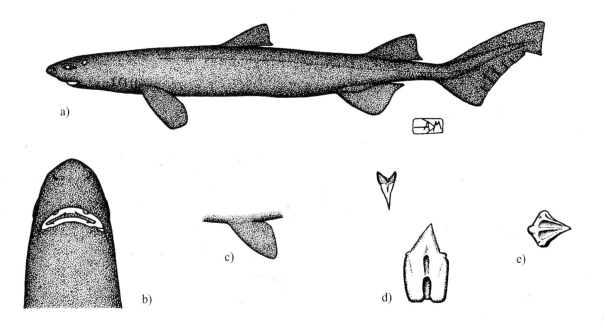

Morphology: Kitefin sharks have a cylindrical and slender body and lack an anal fin. The pectoral fins are short. The dorsal fins begin behind the large pelvic fins; the second dorsal fin is larger than the first. The caudal fin has a short lower lobe and a moderately long upper lobe, with a large terminal lobe. The rear edge of the caudal fin is frayed and lacks a posterior notch. The snout is short and the mouth is almost straight. The eyes, nostrils, and spiracles are all large. There are five pairs of short gill slits located in front of the pectoral fins.

Coloration: Both the dorsal and ventral surfaces are black to brown, sometimes purple. The area around the mouth is white and the pectoral fin is dark on both surfaces. Juveniles may have whitish rear edges on their fins.

Teeth shape: The upper teeth are small, narrow, pointed, and curved, with one cusp. The lower teeth are larger, triangular, with serrated edges, and also with one cusp. These teeth are interlocked to form a cutting wall.

Dental formula: 8–9 : 1 : 7–9 / 8–9 : 1 : 8–9

Diet: Bony fish, sharks, cephalopods, crustaceans, polychaetes, siphonophores, ophiuroids, carcasses

Habitat: Pelagic, mainly in deep water on outer continental and insular shelves and slopes at depths ranging from 133.25 ft to at least 5,905.5 ft

Behavior: Kitefin sharks are active, but timid and generally found alone. They have been classified as facultative ectoparasites, since they obtain sustenance both from external parts of larger organisms (taking bites out of live prey) and from whole smaller prey.

Threat to humans: Not dangerous

Notes: Kitefin sharks are very rare, even on Georges Bank.

Atlantic Angel Shark or Sand Devil Shark

Squatina dumeril (Le Sueur, 1818)

Order:	*Squatiniformes*
Family:	*Squatinidae*
Genus:	*Squatina*
Maximum size:	*5.0 ft*
Size at birth:	*Unknown*
Average size at maturity:	*Male: 3.0–3.5 ft*
	Female: Unknown
Embryonic development:	*Aplacental viviparous*
Gestation:	*Unknown*
Litter size:	*Up to 25*
Maximum age:	*Unknown*
Distribution (area):	*Connecticut, Massachusetts, Rhode Island*
Distribution (world):	*Western Atlantic Ocean*

Atlantic angel shark: a) lateral view, b) ventral view of the head, c) ventral view of the pectoral fin, d) upper and lower teeth, e) placoid scale.

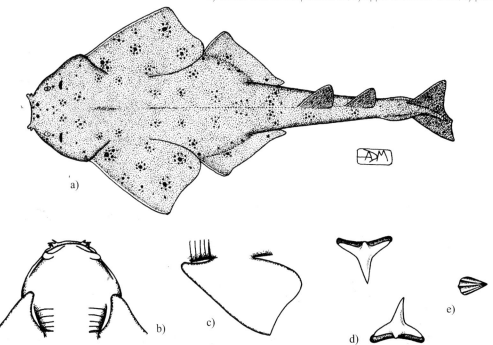

Morphology: Atlantic angel sharks get their name from their distinctive, ray-like, flattened bodies and their very wide head and pectoral and pelvic fins. There is no anal fin and the dorsal fins are located far back. The lower lobe of the caudal fin is larger than the upper lobe, and this shark has caudal keels. The mouth is terminal (located at the end of the snout) and very wide. The eyes are located on the top of the head. As a bottom dweller, this shark has simple, tapering nasal barbels, and the front nasal flaps may be weakly fringed or smooth. The spiracles are large, and there are five pairs of gill slits, all close together and located in front of the pectoral fins. The gills are not visible when the shark rests on the sea bottom.

Coloration: Angel sharks are gray to reddish brown on top, often with small darker spots. Young Atlantic angel sharks often have white spots. Their ventral surfaces are white with red spots and reddish fin margins.

Teeth shape: Both the upper and lower teeth are small and pointed, with one cusp.

Dental formula: 10 : 10 / 9 : 9

Diet: Bony fish, crustaceans, bivalves

Habitat: Benthic, on continental shelves and slopes at depths ranging from the surface to at least 4,560.4 ft.

Behaviour: Solitary and migratory, these sharks bury themselves in the sand (this accounts for their other name, sand devil) of the sea floor, from which they strike at high speed to capture prey with their wide and highly extendable jaws.

Threat to humans: Not dangerous

Notes: The sand devil is common in southern New England waters. Harvesting this species is prohibited, so all sand devils must be released.

(National Marine Fisheries Service, Southeast Fisheries Science Center, Mississippi Laboratories, Pascagoula, Mississippi)

Nurse Shark

Ginglymostoma cirratum (Bonnaterre, 1788)

Order:	*Orectolobiformes*
Family:	*Ginglymostomatidae*
Genus:	*Ginglymostoma*
Maximum size:	*10.0–14.1 ft*
Size at birth:	*10.6–11.8 in*
Average size at maturity:	*Male: 6.9 ft*
	Female: 7.6–7.9 ft
Embryonic development:	*Aplacental viviparous*
Gestation:	*Approx. 5–6 months*
Litter size:	*20–30*
Maximum age:	*25 years*
Distribution (area):	*Connecticut and Rhode Island*
Distribution (world):	*Atlantic and Eastern Pacific Oceans*

Nurse shark: a) lateral view, b) ventral view of the head, c) ventral view of the pectoral fin, d) upper and lower teeth, e) placoid scale.

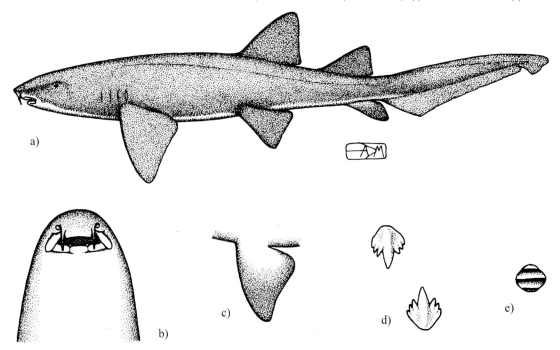

Morphology: Nurse sharks have massive, wide, and rounded heads with a short snout. Their fin tips are rounded. The dorsal fins are located rather far back, over the pelvic fins. The first dorsal fin is moderately large, the second is smaller. The anal fin is smaller than the second dorsal fin, and the pectoral fins are moderately long and wide. The caudal fin has a very short lower lobe and a long upper lobe, with a medium-sized terminal lobe. The mouth is almost straight, with long labial folds. Nurse sharks have long barbels and nasoral grooves around the nostrils. The eyes are small, with strong subocular ridges below them. The spiracles are also small, and there are five pairs of short gill slits, the last three are located over the pectoral fin, and the last two are very close together.

Coloration: Dorsal surfaces are yellow-brown to gray-brown, while ventral surfaces are a light whitish brown. Juveniles may have small, dark, light-ringed spots and very faint saddle-like markings on their backs.

Teeth shape: The upper and lower teeth are relatively small, with one low cusp and four to twelve small cusplets.

Dental formula: 17–18 : 17–18 / 16–17 : 16–17

Diet: Bony fish, rays, crustaceans, sea urchins, cephalopods, algae

Habitat: Benthic, on continental and insular shelves at depths ranging from the surface to at least 426.5 ft

(Claudio Perotti)

Behavior: Nocturnal, nurse sharks are sluggish during the daytime, when they rest on the sandy bottom or in caves. They are solitary or may be found in groups as large as thirty sharks. They can clamber along the bottom using their pectoral fins as limbs. Divers can get fairly close to these sharks without them showing any aggressive behavior. They search for food with their barbels touching the bottom, and use suction to capture or extract prey from crevices and cracks. Nurse sharks can remain motionless, with their snout pointed upward and their body supported off the sea bottom on their pectoral fins (a potential prey may mistake the space under the body of the shark for a place to hide). During mating the male may grab one of the female's pectoral fins with his mouth, which may induce the female to roll on her back on the bottom. The male then inserts a clasper in her vent and rolls on his back to lie motionless beside the female.

Threat to humans: Not dangerous

Notes: Nurse sharks only occasionally stray into Connecticut and Rhode Island waters.

(Joseph Thomas)

Sand Tiger Shark
Carcharias taurus (Rafinesque, 1810)

Order:	*Lamniformes*
Family:	*Odontaspididae*
Genus:	*Carcharias*
Maximum size:	*12.5–14.1 ft*
Size at birth:	*2.9–3.5 ft*
Average size at maturity:	*Male: 6.2–6.4 ft*
	Female: 7.2–7.7 ft
Embryonic development:	*Aplacental viviparous*
Gestation:	*9–2 months*
Litter size:	*2*
Maximum age:	*17 years*
Distribution (area):	*All New England*
Distribution (world):	*Atlantic, Pacific, and Indian Oceans*

Sand tiger shark: a) lateral view, b) ventral view of the head, c) ventral view of the pectoral fin, d) upper and lower teeth, e) placoid scale.

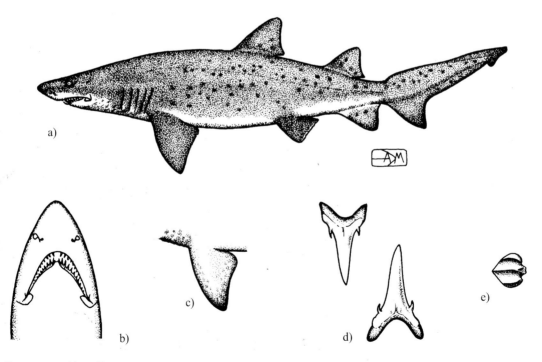

Morphology: Sand tiger sharks have a conical snout that is large and moderately long. The first dorsal fin is large and starts behind the rear tip of the pectoral fin. The second dorsal fin is nearly as large as the first, and the anal fin is about as large as the second dorsal fin. The pectoral fins are wide, but relatively short. The caudal fin has a long upper lobe and a short lower lobe. The body of a sand tiger shark is massive, with a large, short caudal peduncle. The eyes are small and the spiracles are very small. There are five pairs of long gill slits, all located ahead of the pectoral fins.

Coloration: Dorsal surfaces are greenish brown-gray with metallic highlights and yellowish, brownish, or reddish spots. Ventral surfaces are whitish. Sometimes the fin tips and back edges of the fins are dark. The undersurface of the pectoral fin is partially whitish and partially gray-brown; this dark area has indented margins that form patches. The fin tip and back edge are darker.

Teeth shape: Both the upper and lower teeth are long, narrow, and slightly curved, with one cusp and two small cusplets. The teeth of the lower jaw protrude from the mouth and are visible even when the mouth is closed.

(Sarah Taylor / New England Aquarium, Boston, Massachusetts)

Dental formula: 22–24 : 22–24 / 20–23 : 20–23

Diet: Bony fish, elasmobranchs, cephalopods, crustaceans, marine mammals

Habitat: Pelagic, on continental shelves at depths ranging from the surface to at least 885.8 ft

Behavior: Sand tiger sharks are quite active and primarily nocturnal. They may be found alone, in pairs, or in groups of up to 80 or more around a food source or for reproduction. These sharks swallow air at the surface and hold it in their stomach to maintain a relatively neutral buoyancy (they can readily halt and hover motionless in the water). They are migratory and show a social hierarchy, segregating by size and sex. They can be closely approached by divers and usually show no aggressive behavior. They put up little resistance when hooked.

Threat to humans: Potentially dangerous

Notes: Sand tiger sharks visit New England waters only in the summer. This species was once common along southern New England and at the westerly entrance to the Gulf of Maine. They were so abundant that fishing for them was a popular sport. There were commercial fisheries for them around Nantucket in the early twentieth century, but these were short lived, reputedly due to exhaustion of the local stock. Sand tiger sharks are now uncommon in New England waters. Harvesting this species is prohibited and all sand tiger sharks must be released.

Common Thresher Shark

Alopias vulpinus (Bonnaterre, 1788)

Order:	*Lamniformes*
Family:	*Alopiidae*
Genus:	*Alopias*
Maximum size:	*20.9 ft*
Size at birth:	*3.7–5.1 ft*
Average size at maturity:	*Male: 10.5–11.0 ft*
	Female: 12.3–13.8 ft
Embryonic development:	*Aplacental viviparous*
Gestation:	*9 months*
Litter size:	*2–7*
Maximum age:	*19 years*
Distribution (area):	*All New England*
Distribution (world):	*Atlantic, Pacific, and Indian Oceans*

Common thresher shark: a) lateral view, b) ventral view of the head, c) ventral view of the pectoral fin, d) upper and lower teeth, e) placoid scale.

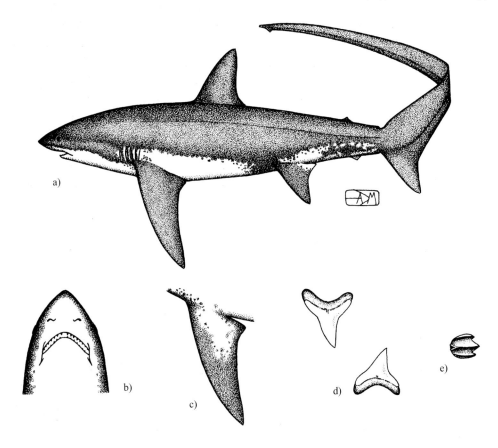

Morphology: Thresher sharks are known for the very long upper lobes on their caudal fins, almost as long as the rest of the body. The lower caudal lobe is relatively short, and this shark has a large caudal penduncle. The pectoral and pelvic fins are long. The first dorsal fin is large, while the second dorsal fin and anal fin are very small. The snout is conical, with a relatively small mouth. The eyes are large, but do not extend up to the dorsal surface of the head. The spiracles are very small, and there are five pairs of short gill slits, the last two located above the base of the pectoral fin.

Coloration: Thresher sharks are dark gray to bluish, with metallic glints on their sides. They are white underneath, except on the pelvic region and caudal peduncle, where the dark coloration extends down and forms an irregular pattern. The boundary separating the top and bottom color patterns is very pronounced on the head. The dark coloration of the dorsal surface extends to the ventral surface of the pectoral fins and there are indented margins forming irregular patches and a white V-shaped area at the base of the pectorals.

Teeth shape: Both the upper and lower teeth have one cusp. They are pointed and oblique, with cutting edges.

Dental formula: 19–26 : 0–1 : 19–26 / 21–24 : 0–1 : 21–24

Diet: Bony fish, cephalopods, crustaceans

Habitat: Pelagic, on continental shelves at depths ranging from the surface to at least 1,200.8 ft. Juveniles are generally found in shallower waters than adults.

Behavior: Thresher sharks have a heat-retaining system, so they are particularly active and fast. They are rather timid and are migratory, and they may be solitary or found in groups, in which they segregate by sex. Threshers can leap out of the water and they use their long upper caudal fin lobes to slash the water in order to herd and disorient the schooling fish on which they prey. They also use the leading edge of their tail to stun prey fish.

Threat to humans: Not dangerous

(Maryland Coast Dispatch)

Notes: Common thresher sharks are relatively abundant in offshore waters as well as in the cold inshore waters of New England and the Gulf of Maine. They are seasonal migrants, occurring in the area from May to October.

Basking Shark
Cetorhinus maximus (Gunnerus, 1765)

Order:	*Lamniformes*
Family:	*Cetorhinidae*
Genus:	*Cetorhinus*
Maximum size:	*32.2–39.4 ft*
Size at birth:	*Approx. 4.9 ft*
Average size at maturity:	*Male: 15.1–19.7 ft*
	Female: 26.3 ft
Embryonic development:	*Aplacental viviparous*
Gestation:	*Unknown (1–3 years)*
Litter size:	*1–6*
Maximum age:	*16 years or more*
Distribution (area):	*All New England*
Distribution (world):	*Atlantic, Pacific, and Indian Oceans*

Basking shark: a) lateral view, b) ventral view of the head, c) ventral view of the pectoral fin, d) upper and lower teeth, e) placoid scale.

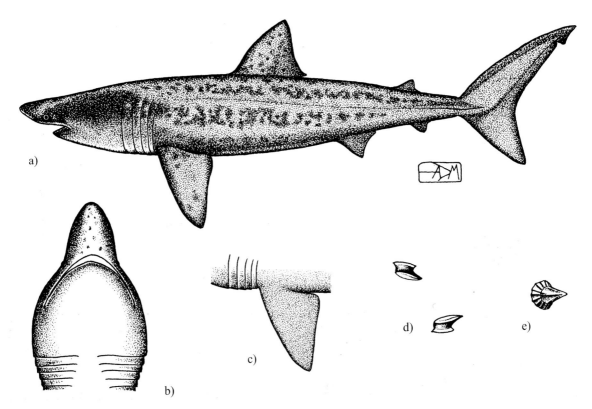

Morphology: The pectoral fins of basking sharks are wide and moderately long. The first dorsal fin is very large and begins behind the rear tip of the pectoral fins. The second dorsal fin is small, and the anal fin is only about as large as the second dorsal fin. The caudal fin is lunate (cresent shaped), with a long upper lobe and relatively short lower lobe. There are wide caudal keels. The snout is long and conical; in juveniles the tip of the snout is narrow and curved. Basking sharks have very wide mouths. There are five pairs of very long gill slits extending from the ventral up to the dorsal surfaces of the head, all located ahead of the pectoral fins. There are gill rakers (bony, finger-like projections that help filter-feeders retain food) present on its internal gill slits. The eyes are small and the spiracles are very small.

Coloration: Basking sharks are brown to gray on their dorsal surface, with irregular dark patches. Their ventral surfaces are similar to the dorsal surfaces, but are sometimes lighter. The undersides of the pectoral fins are dark like the dorsal surface. The ventral surfaces of juveniles are partially white, with the boundary separating dark from white coloration sharp and indented. There have been rare cases of albino basking sharks.

Teeth shape: Both the upper and lower teeth have one cusp and are curved, very small, and very numerous.

Dental formula: Approximately 100 / 100, but with considerable variation

Diet: Planktonic organisms, including crustaceans, bony fish eggs, siphonophores, and jellyfish.

(Greg Sears / Mass Bay Guides)

Habitat: Pelagic, on continental and insular shelves at depths ranging from the surface to at least 1,049.9 ft. A scarcity of pregnant females and newborns seems to suggest that they are segregated from the rest of the populations.

Behavior: Basking sharks usually swim at the surface with their mouths wide open in order to filter the water and capture plankton for food. They are active during the day, but are slow. They may be found alone or in groups—sometimes of more than 500 sharks! They are migratory, and possibly segregate at different water depths by sex. Though they are large, they are able to leap out of the water and may approach divers closely without showing any aggressive behavior. Basking sharks periodically shed their gill rakers in the winter, when plankton levels are low (replacement takes four to five months). During mating, the male places his pectoral fin over the first dorsal fin of the female and swims very close to her while inserting a clasper.

Threat to humans: Not dangerous

Notes: Basking sharks aggregate in the Gulf of Maine from spring through autumn to feed on abundant plankton. Schools of up to fifty have been observed in the southern Gulf in the autumn. They have also been seen in large numbers in late June in Massachusetts Bay. Aerial photographs shot in the southern gulf of Maine show a variety of schooling patterns. The reason for these aggregations remains unknown, but they may represent group courtship behavior. Basking sharks have been seen as close as two miles from shore and they inhabit the entire Massachusetts Bay and the east side of Cape Cod, where they have occasionally been seen breaching in rough seas. Late in the autumn, tagged basking sharks have been recorded moving from temperate feeding areas off the coast of southern New England to the Bahamas, the Caribbean Sea, and even to the coast of South America in the Southern Hemisphere. During the first half of the eighteenth century they were caught in large numbers in Massachusetts waters for their liver oil, which was then in demand as fuel for oil lamps. Today the harvest of basking sharks is prohibited.

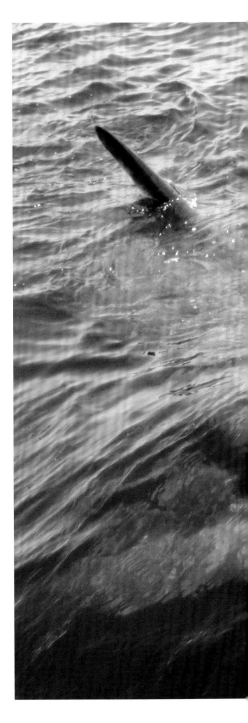

Great White Shark
Carcharodon carcharias (Linnaeus, 1758)

Order:	*Lamniformes*
Family:	*Lamnidae*
Genus:	*Carcharodon*
Maximum size:	*21.9–26.3 ft*
Size at birth:	*3.9–5.0 ft*
Average size at maturity:	*Male: 12.5 ft*
	Female: 14.8–16.4 ft
Embryonic development:	*Aplacental viviparous*
Gestation:	*Unknown*
Litter size:	*2–17*
Maximum age:	*53 years or more*
Distribution (area):	*All New England*
Distribution (world):	*Atlantic, Pacific, and Indian Oceans*

Great white shark: a) lateral view, b) ventral view of the head, c) ventral view of the pectoral fin, d) upper and lower teeth, e) placoid scale.

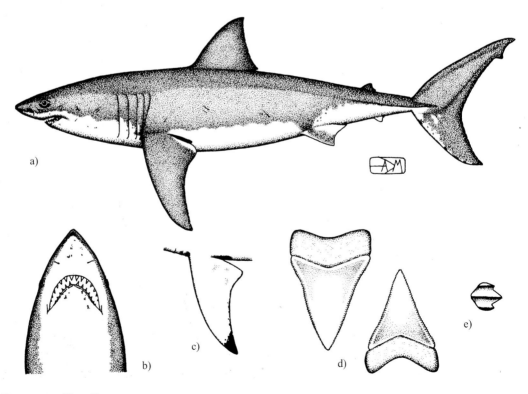

Morphology: Great white sharks have a massive body with a large and conical snout. The mouth is wide and the eyes are moderately large. The caudal fin is lunate, or crescent shaped, with a long upper lobe and slightly shorter lower lobe. The first dorsal fin is large and the second is very small. The anal fin is about as large as the second dorsal fin. The pectoral fins are wide and long, and great whites have wide caudal keels. Their spiracles are very small or may be absent. There are five pairs of long gill slits, all located ahead of the pectoral fins.

Coloration: The dorsal surfaces of great whites are grayish brown; the flanks are usually lighter colored than the top. The undersides are white, giving them their name. The boundary line separating the top and bottom coloration is very distinct. The undersurfaces of the pectoral fins show a black patch at the tip and a narrow black band on the trailing edge, with some small black spots. At the base of the pectoral fin is a black or gray patch. The eyes are dark. There have been rare cases of albino great whites.

Teeth shape: The triangular upper teeth have one cusp and are large and wide with strongly serrated edges. The lower teeth are similar to the uppers, but narrower. The lower teeth protrude from the mouth and are visible even when the shark's mouth is closed. Newborn great whites have two very small cusplets, in both the upper and lower teeth, and the lower teeth are not serrated.

(Vittorio Gabriotti)

Dental formula: 12–14 : 12–14 / 10–13 : 10–13

Diet: Bony fish, elasmobranchs, marine mammals, mollusks, crustaceans, sea turtles, birds, carcasses.

Habitat: Pelagic, mainly on continental and insular shelves at depths ranging from the surface to at least 4,199.5 ft.

Behavior: Equally diurnal and nocturnal, great whites have a heat-retaining system, so they are particularly active and fast; and they are strong, able to leap out of the water. Normally solitary, they may be seen in pairs or in groups around a food source. They are migratory and may segregate by size or gender, possibly even by water depth. They also show a social hierarchy when feeding. Great whites might approach divers closely, often without showing any aggressive behavior. They have been seen to perform a threat display with their jaws slightly open and their pectoral fins depressed. They have been seen raising their head out of water in order to observe an object of interest, and they are even known to ingest items that are inedible. Great whites use predatory tactics that enable them to eat their prey with minimal risk of injury and minimal energy expenditure. They may attack either horizontally or vertically by swimming rapidly from deep waters. The initial attack is by surprise and usually not immediately fatal to the prey. The great white shark will swim off and wait while the stunned prey dies from blood loss. Then the shark returns minutes later to consume the prey. During mating, the male and female stay belly to belly while the male inserts the clasper.

Threat to humans: Highly dangerous

Notes: The popular film *Jaws* gave great whites the reputation as a man-eater. Yet, while these sharks do sometimes attack people, occasionally even boats, they do not generally target or hunt humans specifically. Most attacks by great whites on people end as soon as the shark realizes what it has bitten and releases the prey. Even though great white sharks are relatively uncommon, they occur regularly in New England waters. Historically, in the region south of Cape Elizabeth, Maine, great whites were often caught by fishermen and were regularly present at floating whale carcasses. The New York Bight is an important nursery ground for great whites in the western North Atlantic. Harvesting of great whites is prohibited.

Shortfin Mako Shark
Isurus oxyrinchus (Rafinesque, 1809)

Order:	*Lamniformes*
Family:	*Lamnidae*
Genus:	*Isurus*
Maximum size:	*14.6 ft*
Size at birth:	*2.0–2.3 ft*
Average size at maturity:	*Male: 6.4 ft*
	Female: 9.0–9.8 ft
Embryonic development:	*Aplacental viviparous*
Gestation:	*15–18 months*
Litter size:	*4–25*
Maximum age:	*25–45 years*
Distribution (area):	*All New England*
Distribution (world):	*Atlantic, Pacific, and Indian Oceans*

Shortfin mako shark: a) lateral view, b) ventral view of the head, c) ventral view of the pectoral fin, d) upper and lower teeth, e) placoid scale.

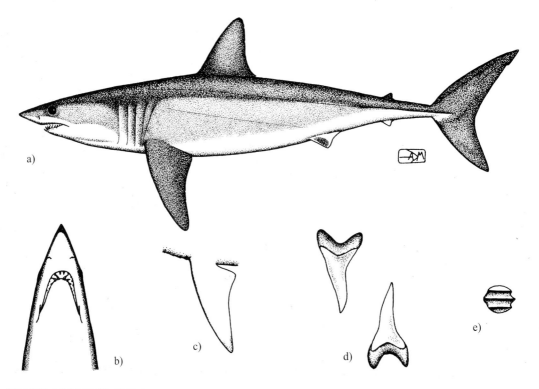

Morphology: Shortfin makos have very spindle-shaped bodies. They are quite slender when young, but adults are more massive. The snout is conical, narrow, long, and strongly pointed. The first dorsal fin is tall and located behind the rear tip of the pectoral fin. The second dorsal fin is very small, and the anal fin is about as large as the second dorsal fin. The pectoral fins are relatively short (about 70% of the head length). The caudal fin is lunate, with a long upper lobe and a lower lobe that is slightly shorter. There are wide caudal keels. The mouth is long, but sharply curved, so it is narrow when seen from below. The eyes are relatively large, and the spiracles are very small. There are five pairs of long gill slits, all located in front of the pectoral fin.

Coloration: Shortfin mako sharks have brilliant blue to black dorsal surfaces with pronounced iridescence on the sides. Their undersides are white and the boundary separating the dorsal and ventral coloration is quite distinct. Sometimes, the underside of the pectoral fin shows a small, light grayish area at the apex and posterior margin. These sharks have black eyes.

Teeth shape: The upper teeth are large, narrow, long, and curved. They have one cusp and cutting edges. The lower teeth are similar, but they protrude from the mouth and are visible even when the shark's mouth is closed.

(Jessica Heim)

Dental formula: 12–14 : 12–14 / 11–15 : 11–15

Diet: Bony fish, elasmobranchs, marine turtles, squids, crustaceans, marine mammals, birds, salps, porifera, carcasses

Habitat: Pelagic, on continental and insular shelves, upper slopes, and ocean basins at depths ranging from the surface to at least 1,368.1 ft. Juveniles may be found in shallower waters.

Behavior: Shortfin makos have a heat-retaining system, so they are particularly active and fast, and may even leap clear of the water. They are migratory and may be found alone or in large groups. They are rather timid and rarely approach divers closely. They can be quite aggressive, though they sometimes approach without showing any aggressive behavior. Shortfin makos segregate by size and demonstrate a social hierarchy when feeding. They will occasionally ingest inedible items. Shortfin makos are nervous and perform threat displays that include gaping its lower jaw slightly and turning in figure-eights as they swim closer to the threat. It is possible that their attacks on prey are both horizontally or vertically oriented. Shortfin makos are one of the fastest sharks and can easily outswim most prey.

Threat to humans: Dangerous

Notes: Shortfin mako sharks are common in offshore waters south of Cape Cod, Massachusetts. They are commonly caught by commercial and sport fishermen.

(Jessica Heim)

Porbeagle
Lamna nasus (Bonnaterre, 1788)

Order:	*Lamniformes*
Family:	*Lamnidae*
Genus:	*Lamna*
Maximum size:	*11.8 ft*
Size at birth:	*2.0–2.9 ft*
Average size at maturity:	*Male: 6.2–7.1 ft*
	Female: 6.6–8.9 ft
Embryonic development:	*Aplacental viviparous*
Gestation:	*8–9 months*
Litter size:	*2–6*
Maximum age:	*29–46 years*
Distribution (area):	*All New England*
Distribution (world):	*Atlantic, Pacific, and Indian Oceans*

Porbeagle: a) lateral view, b) ventral view of the head, c) ventral view of the pectoral fin, d) upper and lower teeth, e) placoid scale.

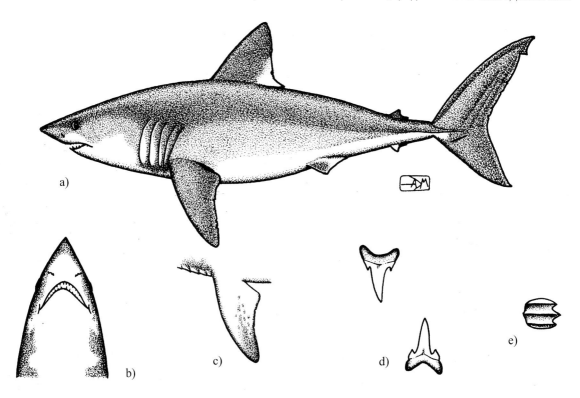

Morphology: Porbeagles have spindle-shaped bodies that are stout and massive, with conical, pointed snouts. The caudal fin is lunate, with a long upper lobe and slightly shorter lower lobe. The first dorsal fin is quite large and is situated over the inner margin of the pectoral fin. The second dorsal fin is very small, and the anal fin is about as large as the second dorsal fin. The pectoral fins are relatively short, and there are two pairs of caudal keels, one wider pair on the caudal peduncle and a smaller pair on the sides of the caudal fin, immediately below the peduncle. The mouth is relatively small, and the eyes are large. The spiracles are very small or may be absent. There are five pairs of long gill slits, all located in front of the pectoral fin origin.

Coloration: The dorsal surfaces of porbeagles are bluish gray to black. The ventral surfaces are generally white, except around the gill slits, which sometimes show irregular dark spots. The rear tip of the first dorsal fin has a conspicuous white patch. The underside of the pectoral fins has a dark area extending from the tip toward the body and there are indented margins that form small spots. The boundary separating the dorsal and ventral coloration is sharp and indented.

Teeth shape: Both the upper and lower teeth are relatively small, with one cusp having cutting edges and two small cusplets. The teeth of the lower jaw protrude from the mouth and are visible even when the mouth is closed. The teeth of juvenile porbeagles may lack cusplets.

Dental formula: 12–16 : 12–16 / 7–13 : 7–13

Diet: Bony fish, sharks, squids, birds

Habitat: Pelagic, on continental shelves and ocean basins at depths ranging from the surface to at least 1,213.9 ft.

Behavior: Porbeagles have heat-retaining systems and they are particularly active and very fast swimmers that are able to leap out of the water. They may be solitary or found in large groups. They are rather timid and are migratory. Porbeagles segregate by size and sex.

Threat to humans: Potentially dangerous

Notes: The porbeagle is common from southwest of the Grand Banks to Massachusetts Bay. Its liver oil, mixed with other fish oils, was prized during the first quarter of the nineteenth century for use in tanning leather. Porbeagles are routinely caught by both commercial and sport fishermen.

Iceland Catshark

Apristurus laurussoni (Saemundsson, 1922)

Order:	*Carcharhiniformes*
Family:	*Scyliorhinidae*
Genus:	*Apristurus*
Maximum size:	*2.2 ft*
Size at birth:	*Unknown*
Average size at maturity:	*Male: Unknown*
	Female: Unknown
Embryonic development:	*Probably oviparous*
Gestation:	*Unknown*
Litter size:	*Unknown*
Maximum age:	*Unknown*
Distribution (area):	*Massachusetts, though not common*
Distribution (world):	*Atlantic Ocean*

Iceland catshark: a) lateral view, b) ventral view of the head, c) ventral view of the pectoral fin, d) upper and lower teeth, e) placoid scale.

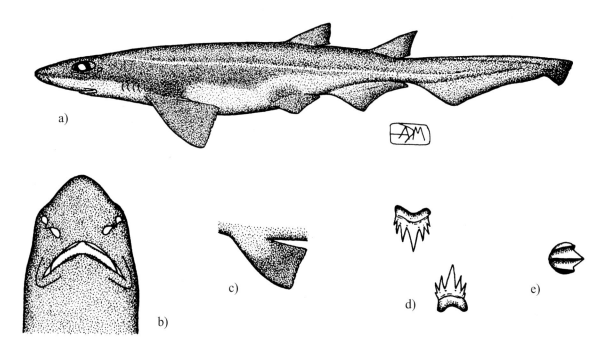

Morphology: Iceland catsharks have an elongated and slender body with a long, flattened snout. The dorsal fins are located fairly far back. They are small and of similar size and are situated above the pelvic fins. The caudal fin has a very short lower lobe and a moderately long upper lobe that is elongated along the axis of the body and has a relatively wide terminal lobe. The anal fin is long, reaching the base of the caudal fin. The pectoral fins are short and small. The eyes are large, and the nostrils are very wide, their width is nearly one and a half times greater than the space between the nostrils. The labial folds are long, and the spiracles are relatively small. There are five pairs of short gill slits, the fifth is located over the base of the pectoral fin.

Coloration: The dorsal surfaces are dark brown with much lighter ventral coloration.

Teeth shape: Both the upper and lower teeth are very small, with one cusp and two to four cusplets, and with smooth edges.

Dental formula: 35–45 : 35–45 / 27–37 : 27–36

Maximum age: Unknown

Diet: Unknown

Habitat: Benthic, in deep water on upper continental slopes at depths ranging from 1,837.3 ft to at least 6,758.5 ft.

Behavior: Unknown

Threat to humans: Not dangerous

Notes: Because they live on the deep ocean floor, not a lot is known about the Iceland catshark, and photographs of this elusive shark are uncommon.

(Andrey Dolgov / PINRO)

Ghost Catshark
Apristurus manis (Springer, 1979)

Order:	*Carcharhiniformes*
Family:	*Scyliorhinidae*
Genus:	*Apristurus*
Maximum size:	*2.8 t*
Size at birth:	*Unknown*
Average size at maturity:	*Male: Unknown*
	Female: Unknown
Embryonic development:	*Oviparous*
Gestation:	*Unknown*
Litter size:	*Unknown*
Maximum age:	*Unknown*
Distribution (area):	*Massachusetts, though not common*
Distribution (world):	*Atlantic Ocean*

Ghost catshark: a) lateral view, b) ventral view of the head, c) ventral view of the pectoral fin, d) upper and lower teeth.

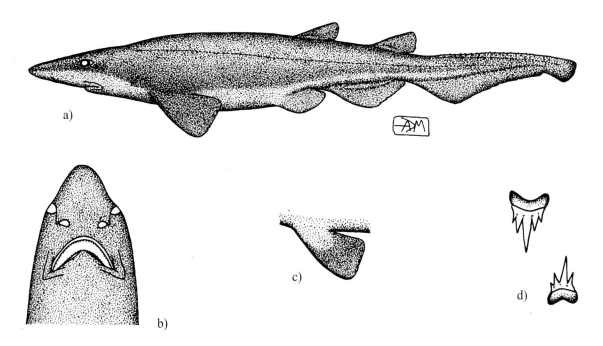

Morphology: Ghost catsharks have a stout body with a pronounced dorsal region and a long, flattened snout. The dorsal fins are located far back over the pelvic fins. The first dorsal fin is small and the second is slightly larger. The caudal fin has a very short lower lobe and a moderately long upper lobe that is elongated on the axis of the body and has a relatively wide terminal lobe. There is a prominent crest of enlarged denticles along the front edge of the caudal fin upper lobe. The anal fin is long and reaches the base of the caudal fin. The pectoral fins are short and small. The eyes are small, and the nostrils are very wide, each slightly larger than the width between them. The labial folds are long, and the spiracles are relatively small. There are five pairs of short gill slits, the fifth is located over the pectoral fin base.

Coloration: Dorsal surfaces are light gray to blackish, with ventral surfaces that are light gray.

Teeth shape: Both upper and lower teeth are very small, with one cusp and two to four cusplets, with smooth edges.

Dental formula: 30 : 30 / 26 : 26

Diet: Unknown

Habitat: Benthic, in deep water on continental slopes at depths ranging from 2,158.8 ft to at least 5,708.7 ft.

Behavior: Unknown

Threat to humans: Not dangerous

Notes: As with its cousin, the Iceland catshark, not much is known about the ghost catshark.

A 2.1-ft ghost catshark caught in the Western North Atlantic and preserved at the Museum of Comparative Zoology of the Harvard University in Cambridge, Massachusetts, with cat. no. MCZ 158894.

Black Roughscale Catshark

Apristurus melanoasper (Iglésias, Nakaya, and Stehmann, 2004)

Order:	Carcharhiniformes
Family:	Scyliorhinidae
Genus:	Apristurus
Maximum size:	2.5 ft
Size at birth:	Unknown
Average size at maturity:	Male: 2.0–2.1 ft
	Female: 1.8–1.9 ft
Embryonic development:	Oviparous
Gestation:	Unknown
Litter size:	1
Maximum age:	Unknown
Distribution (area):	Georges Bank, though not common
Distribution (world):	Atlantic Ocean

Black roughscale catshark: a) lateral view, b) ventral view of the head, c) ventral view of the pectoral fin, d) upper and lower teeth, e) placoid scale.

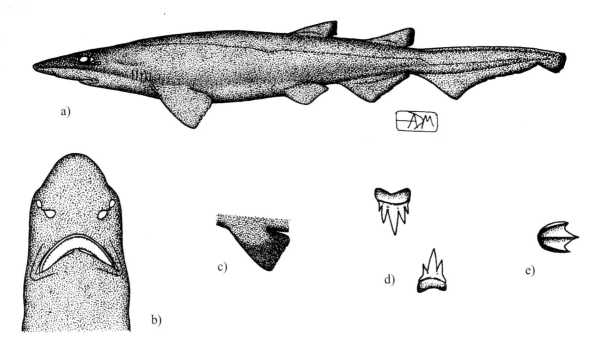

Morphology: As with other catsharks, the black roughscale has a relatively stout body, a long, flattened snout, and dorsal fins located far back over the pelvic fins. The first dorsal fin is small and the second is slightly larger. The caudal fin has a very short lower lobe and a moderately long upper lobe that is elongated on the axis of the body and has a relatively wide terminal lobe. The anal fin is long and reaches the base of the caudal fin. The pectoral fins are short and small. The eyes are moderately large, and the nostrils are very wide, about equal to the space between them. The labial folds are long, and the spiracles are relatively small. There are five pairs of short gill slits, the fifth is located above the base of the pectoral fin.

Coloration: Black roughscale catsharks are dark over their entire bodies. They are generally black to brownish in color.

Teeth shape: The upper teeth are very small, having one cusp and two to four cusplets, with smooth edges. The lower teeth are similar, but have one cusp and only two cusplets.

Dental formula: Unknown

Embryonic development: Oviparous. Their eggs are 2.1 to 2.6 in long, 0.9 to 1.1 in wide, and are furnished with long tendrils.

Diet: Unknown

Habitat: Benthic, in deep water on continental slopes at depths ranging from 1,679.8 ft to at least 4,986.9 ft.

Behavior: Unknown

Threat to humans: Not dangerous

Notes: As with other deep-dwelling catsharks, not a lot is known about the black roughscale catshark.

A 2.3-ft male black roughscale catshark caught in the Western North Atlantic and preserved at the Museum of Comparative Zoology of the Harvard University in Cambridge, Massachusetts, with cat. no. MCZ 165144.

Deepwater Catshark

Apristurus profundorum (Goode & Bean, 1896)

Order:	*Carcharhiniformes*
Family:	*Scyliorhinidae*
Genus:	*Apristurus*
Maximum size:	*1.7 ft or more*
Size at birth:	*Unknown*
Average size at maturity:	*Male: Unknown*
	Female: Unknown
Embryonic development:	*Probably oviparous*
Gestation:	*Unknown*
Litter size:	*Unknown*
Maximum age:	*Unknown*
Distribution (area):	*Rhode Island, near Bear Seamount, Massachusetts*
Distribution (world):	*Atlantic Ocean*

Deepwater catshark: a) lateral view, b) ventral view of the head, c) ventral view of the pectoral fin, d) upper and lower teeth, e) placoid scale.

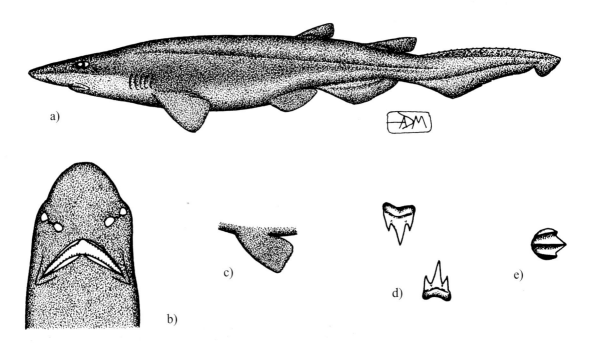

a)

b)

c)

d)

e)

Morphology: Like their cousins, deepwater catsharks have a long, flattened snout and, in deepwater catsharks, the snout is also rather thick. They have relatively stout bodies, with a pronounced dorsal part. The dorsal fins are located far back, originating over the pelvic fins. The first dorsal fin is small, the second is slightly larger. The caudal fin has a very short lower lobe and a moderately long upper lobe that is elongated on the axis of the body and has a relatively wide terminal lobe. The front edge of the caudal fin has a prominent crest of enlarged dermal denticles. The anal fin is long, reaching the base of the caudal fin, and the pectoral fins are short and small. The eyes are moderately large, and the nostrils are very wide—their width is about 1.2 times larger than the space between them. The labial folds are long, and the spiracles are relatively large. There are five pairs of relatively short gill slits, the fifth is positioned over the pectoral fin base.

Coloration: Both the dorsal and ventral surfaces are dark brown to blackish.

Teeth shape: Both the upper and lower teeth are very small, with one cusp, two cusplets, and smooth edges.

Dental formula: 25 : 25 / 25 : 25

Diet: Unknown

Habitat: Benthic, in deep water on continental slopes at depths ranging from 3,280.8 ft to at least 5,249.3 ft.

Behavior: Unknown

Threat to humans: Not dangerous

Notes: Because of the depths at which these sharks live, not much is known about them.

A deepwater catshark caught near Bear Seamount, Massachusetts, and preserved at the Yale Peabody Museum of Natural History in New Haven, Connecticut, with cat. no. YPM 11269. (Gregory J. Watkins-Colwell)

Chain Catshark
Scyliorhinus retifer (Garman, 1881)

Order:	*Carcharhiniformes*
Family:	*Scyliorhinidae*
Genus:	*Scyliorhinus*
Maximum size:	*1.9 ft*
Size at birth:	*3.9–4.3 in*
Average size at maturity:	*Male: 1.2–1.6 ft*
	Female: 1.2–1.7 ft
Embryonic development:	*Oviparous*
Gestation:	*7 months (egg case hatching)*
Litter size:	*2*
Maximum age:	*Unknown*
Distribution (area):	*All New England*
Distribution (world):	*Western Atlantic Ocean*

Chain catshark: a) lateral view, b) ventral view of the head, c) ventral view of the pectoral fin, d) upper and lower teeth, e) placoid scale.

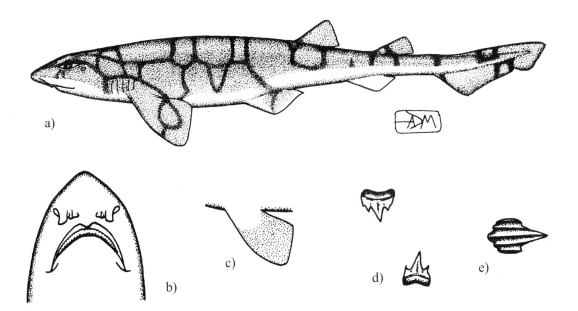

Morphology: Unlike other catsharks, which have stout bodies, the body of the chain catshark is elongated and slender and has a short, flattened snout. The dorsal fins are located far back, beginning just behind the pelvic fins. The first dorsal fin is small and the second is slightly smaller still. The caudal fin lacks a posterior notch and both lobes of the caudal are short, though the upper lobe is elongated with a wide terminal lobe. The anal fin is slightly larger than the second dorsal fin, and the pectoral fins are short. The eyes are relatively large, and the nostrils are wide. The labial folds are short, and the spiracles are relatively small. There are five pairs of short gill slits, the fourth and fifth are located above the base of the pectoral fin.

Coloration: The dorsal surfaces of the chain catshark are reddish brown and have black lines outlining dusky saddles and sometimes forming a chainlike pattern that gives the shark its name. The ventral surfaces are yellowish in color.

Teeth shape: Both the upper and lower teeth are very small, with one cusp and two cusplets, with smooth edges.

Dental formula: 21–26 : 0–2 : 21–26 / 20–22 : 0–4 : 20–22

Embryonic development: Oviparous. Their eggs are 2.6 in long, 1.1 in wide, and are furnished with long tendrils.

Diet: Bony fish, squids, polychaetes, crustaceans

Habitat: Benthic, mainly in deep water on outer continental shelves and upper slopes at depths ranging from 239.5 ft to at least 2,473.8 ft.

(Sarah Taylor / New England
Aquarium, Boston, Massachusetts)

Behavior: Unknown

Threat to humans: Not dangerous

Notes: Chain catsharks are relatively common in New England waters, and are more abundant in Massachusetts and on Georges Bank.

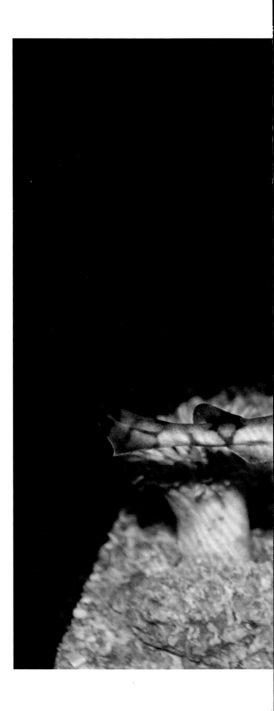

Dusky Smoothhound
Mustelus canis (Mitchell, 1815)

Order:	*Carcharhiniformes*
Family:	*Triakidae*
Genus:	*Mustelus*
Maximum size:	*4.9 ft*
Size at birth:	*1.1–1.3 ft*
Average size at maturity:	*Male: 2.7 ft*
	Female: 3.0 ft
Embryonic development:	*Placental viviparous*
Gestation:	*Approx. 10 months*
Litter size:	*4–20*
Maximum age:	*Unknown*
Distribution (area):	*All New England*
Distribution (world):	*Western Atlantic Ocean*

Dusky smoothhound: a) lateral view, b) ventral view of the head, c) ventral view of the pectoral fin, d) upper and lower teeth, e) placoid scale.

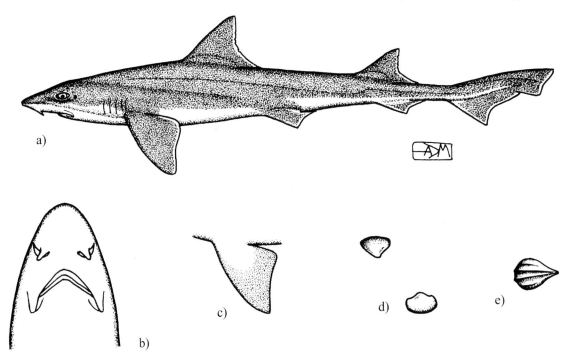

Morphology: Dusky smoothhounds have slender bodies with a long snout that is strongly flattened on the underside. The first dorsal fin is relatively large and located over the pectoral fins. The second dorsal fin is slightly smaller, and the anal fin is much smaller than the second dorsal fin. The pectoral fins are relatively short, but rather wide. The caudal fin has a very short lower lobe and a moderately long upper lobe with a large terminal lobe. The eyes are large and located near the top of the head. The nostrils are wide, the labial folds are relatively short, and the spiracles are medium size. There are five pairs of short gill slits, the last two located over the base of the pectoral fin.

Coloration: Dusky smoothhounds are olive gray to brown on top, with yellowish or grayish white undersides. The tips of the dorsal fins and the upper lobe of the caudal fin are usually dark colored in young sharks.

Teeth shape: Both the upper and lower teeth are small, with one cusp and a very low profile.

Dental formula: Unknown

Diet: Crustaceans, bony fish, molluscs, annelid worms

Habitat: Benthic, on continental and insular shelves and upper slopes at depths ranging from the surface to at least 1,889.7 ft. These sharks are able to live in fresh water for short periods of time.

A dusky smoothhound feeding on a longfin inshore squid (*Loligo pealei*). The photo was taken at the Marine Biological Laboratory in Woods Hole, Massachusetts.

(Jayne M. Gardiner)

Behavior: Dusky smoothhound sharks are active and migratory. They also show a social hierarchy. This species is constantly patroling the seabed for food.

Threat to humans: Not dangerous

Notes: This is the second most abundant shark off southern New England, though its numbers fall far short of the piked dogfish. It has been estimated that in Buzzards Bay, Massachusetts, at the turn of the century, these sharks consumed 200,000 crabs, 60,000 lobsters, and 70,000 small fish annually.

Atlantic Weasel Shark

Paragaleus pectoralis (Garman, 1906)

Order:	*Carcharhiniformes*
Family:	*Hemigaleidae*
Genus:	*Paragaleus*
Maximum size:	*4.5 ft*
Size at birth:	*1.5 ft*
Average size at maturity:	*Male: 2.6 ft*
	Female: 2.5–3.0 ft
Embryonic development:	*Placental viviparous*
Gestation:	*Unknown*
Litter size:	*1–4*
Maximum age:	*Unknown*
Distribution (area):	*Southern New England*
Distribution (world):	*Tropical eastern Atlantic Ocean, off Africa*

Atlantic weasel shark: a) lateral view, b) ventral view of the head, c) ventral view of the pectoral fin, d) upper and lower teeth, e) placoid scale.

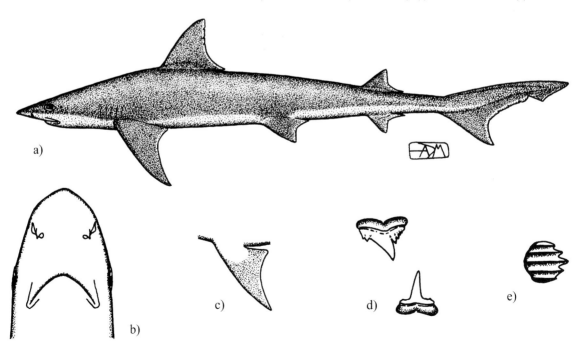

Morphology: Atlantic weasel sharks have slender bodies with long snouts that are flattened on the underside. The first dorsal fin is moderately large, starting above the rear tip of the pectoral fin. The second dorsal fin is smaller than the first, and the anal fin is smaller than the second dorsal fin. The pectoral fins are narrow and relatively short. The caudal fin has a short lower lobe and a moderately long upper lobe with a large terminal lobe. The eyes are large, the nostrils are wide, and the labial folds are relatively short. The spiracles are small, and there are five pairs of short gill slits, the last two located above the pectoral fin.

Coloration: Atlantic weasel sharks are light olive gray or bronze, with yellow lengthwise bands. Their undersides and the rear edges of their fins are lighter in color.

Teeth shape: The upper teeth have one cusp that is pointed and oblique and with two to six small cusplets, mostly located on the lateral margin. The lower front teeth have one cusp that is narrow, pointed, erect, and with smooth edges. The other lower teeth are similar to the upper teeth, but smaller.

Dental formula: 12–13 : 3 : 12–13 / 13–15 : 3 : 13–15

Diet: Cephalopods, bony fish

Habitat: Pelagic, on continental shelves at depths ranging from the surface to at least 328.1 ft.

Behavior: Unknown

Threat to humans: Not dangerous

Notes: There is only one record of an Atlantic weasel shark off southern New England. This specimen may have crossed the Atlantic on the North Equatorial Current and rode the Gulf Stream up to where it was caught in New England. While there is suitable tropical habitat for this shark in the western Atlantic, and such habitat has been extensively surveyed, there have been no other records of it from anywhere in the tropical western Atlantic. It is possible that a common, wide-ranging eastern Atlantic shark such as this species has an undiscovered related population in the western Atlantic.

Silky Shark
Carcharhinus falciformis (Bibron, 1839)

Order:	*Carcharhiniformes*
Family:	*Carcharhinidae*
Genus:	*Carcharhinus*
Maximum size:	*10.8 ft*
Size at birth:	*2.1–2.5 ft*
Average size at maturity:	*Male: 6.0–7.1 ft*
	Female: 5.9–7.6 ft
Embryonic development:	*Placental viviparous*
Gestation:	*Approx. 12 months*
Litter size:	*2–15*
Maximum age:	*12 years or more*
Distribution (area):	*Southern New England*
Distribution (world):	*Atlantic, Pacific, and Indian Oceans*

Silky shark: a) lateral view, b) ventral view of the head, c) ventral view of the pectoral fin, d) upper and lower teeth, e) placoid scale.

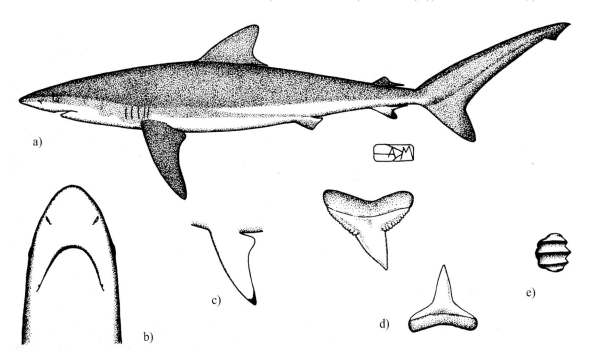

Morphology: Silky sharks have relatively slender bodies with snouts that are long and flattened, yet rounded in the front. The first dorsal fin begins behind the pectorals and is moderately large, the second dorsal fin is small. The anal fin is about as large as the second dorsal fin; it has a long tip and the back edge is deeply concave. The pelvic fins are very small and the pectorals are relatively short. The caudal fin has a relatively short lower lobe with a slightly rounded tip and a long upper lobe with a medium-size terminal lobe. Silky sharks have a pronounced interdorsal ridge (ridge of skin running between the two dorsal fins). Their mouths are wide and curved when seen from below. The labial folds are short. The eyes and nostrils are relatively small and there are no spiracles. There are five pairs of short gill slits, the last two located over the pectoral fins.

Coloration: The dorsal surfaces of silky sharks are grayish brown to blackish, with an inconspicuous white band on the flanks. The underside is white. The tips of the fins are darker, and this is more evident on the anal fin. The underside of the pectoral fin, while white in color, has a small, sharply defined black patch at the tips.

Teeth shape: The upper teeth have one cusp, that is narrow, pointed, oblique, and has serrated edges. The lower teeth have one cusp and are smaller, narrow, pointed, and erect to oblique, with cutting edges.

Dental formula: 15–16 : 2 : 15–16 / 15–16 : 1–2 : 15–16

Diet: Bony fish, elasmobranchs, cephalopods, crustaceans, carcasses

Habitat: Pelagic, on continental and insular shelves, upper slopes, and ocean basins at depths ranging from the surface to at least 1,640.4 ft.

(Harald Bänsch)

Behavior: Silky sharks are nocturnal and they are fast and very active in their search for food. They are solitary or may be found in groups, where they segregate by size. They might approach divers closely, usually without showing any aggressive behavior. When alarmed, they perform a threat display with the back arched, snout lifted, and caudal fin depressed.

Threat to humans: Potentially dangerous

Notes: A largely tropical species, silky sharks are uncommon in those New England waters where they have been reported. Harvest of this species is prohibited.

(Johan Lantz)

Bull Shark

Carcharhinus leucas (Valenciennes, 1839)

Order:	*Carcharhiniformes*
Family:	*Carcharhinidae*
Genus:	*Carcharhinus*
Maximum size:	*11.2 ft*
Size at birth:	*1.8–2.7 ft*
Average size at maturity:	*Male: 5.2–7.4 ft*
	Female: 5.9–7.6 ft
Embryonic development:	*Placental viviparous*
Gestation:	*10–11 months*
Litter size:	*1–13*
Maximum age:	*25 years or more*
Distribution (area):	*Southern New England*
Distribution (world):	*Atlantic, Pacific, and Indian Oceans*

Bull shark: a) lateral view, b) ventral view of the head, c) ventral view of the pectoral fin, d) upper and lower teeth, e) placoid scale.

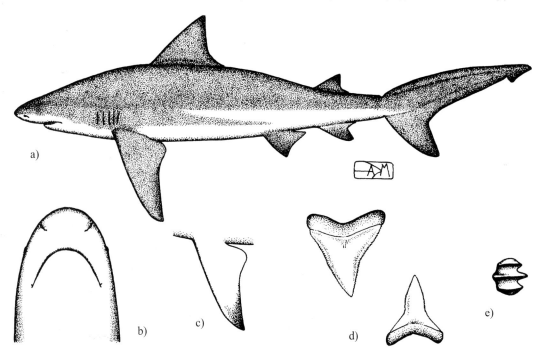

Morphology: Bull sharks have a massive and stout body with a short, flattened snout that appears rounded in the front. There is a pronounced dorsal rise behind the head. The first dorsal fin is large, erect, and pointed. The second dorsal fin is small, and the anal fin is about as large as the second dorsal fin. The pectoral fins are pointed, moderately long, and falcate (curved slightly). The caudal fin has a relatively short lower lobe and a long upper lobe with a medium-size terminal lobe. The mouth is wide and curved when view from below. The labial folds are short, and both the eyes and nostrils are small. There are five pairs of short gill slits, the last two located over the pectoral fin.

Coloration: Bull sharks are gray on their dorsal surfaces, with an inconspicuous whitish band on their flanks. Their undersides are white, though the tips of the pectoral fins have dark patches.

Teeth shape: The upper teeth have one cusp and are erect to oblique, with strongly serrated edges. The lower teeth also have one cusp, but are smaller, narrow, pointed, erect, and with very finely serrated edges.

Dental formula: 12–14 : 12–14 / 12–13 : 12–13

Diet: Bony fish, elasmobranchs, turtles, mammals, crustaceans, molluscs, sea urchins, birds, carcasses

Habitat: Pelagic, on continental and insular shelves at depths ranging from the surface to at least 498.7 ft. These sharks can live in fresh water for long periods of time (there are recorded sightings of them in the Mississippi River). Pregnant females give birth close inshore, where juveniles remain, while males stay in deeper water.

(Claudio Perotti)

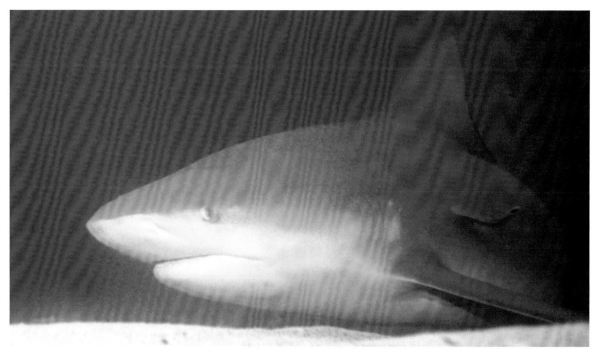

Behavior: Bull sharks are active and fast. They are solitary, but sometimes hunt in pairs, or may be found in groups around a food source. Young bull sharks can leap and spin out of the water. They can approach divers closely, often without showing any aggressive behavior. They occasionally ingest inedible items.

Threat to humans: Highly dangerous. They are one of the three species (including tiger and great white sharks) that are most likely to attack humans.

Notes: Uncommon in the New England waters where they've been recorded.

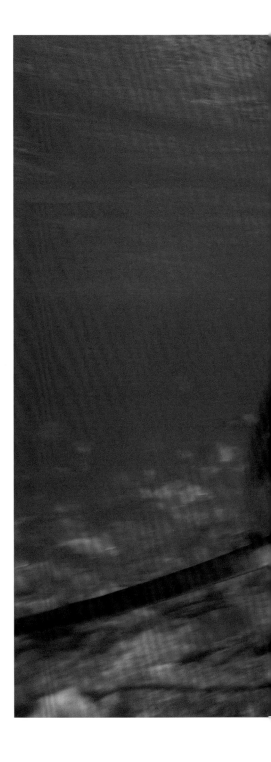

Blacktip Shark

Carcharhinus limbatus (Valenciennes, 1839)

Order:	*Carcharhiniformes*
Family:	*Carcharhinidae*
Genus:	*Carcharhinus*
Maximum size:	*8.4 ft*
Size at birth:	*1.36–2.4 ft*
Average size at maturity:	*Male: 5.3–6.6 ft*
	Female: 4.8–5.6 ft
Embryonic development:	*Placental viviparous*
Gestation:	*12 months*
Litter size:	*1–10*
Maximum age:	*10 years or more*
Distribution (area):	*Southern New England*
Distribution (world):	*Atlantic, Pacific, and Indian Oceans*

Blacktip shark: a) lateral view, b) ventral view of the head, c) ventral view of the pectoral fin, d) upper and lower teeth, e) placoid scale.

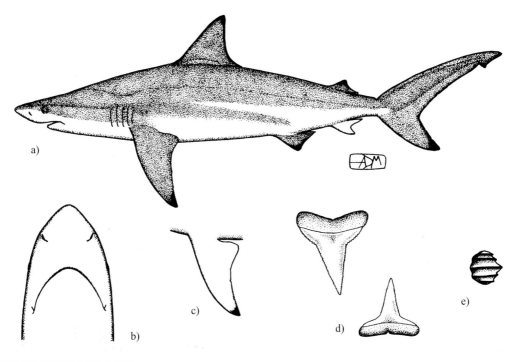

Morphology: Blacktip sharks have long, flattened snouts and a pronounced dorsal rise behind their heads. The first dorsal fin is pointed and erect. It is fairly large and usually quite tall, and narrow at the top. The second dorsal fin is small, and the anal fin is about as large as the second dorsal fin, with the posterior margin not deeply concave. The pectoral fins are perfectly falcate, pointed, and moderately long. The caudal fin has a relatively short lower lobe and a long upper lobe with a medium-size terminal lobe. Their mouths are wide and parabolic when viewed from beneath. The labial folds are short, and the eyes and nostrils are small. This species has no spiracles. There are five pairs of short gill slits, the last two located above the base of the pectoral fin.

Coloration: The dorsal surfaces of blacktip sharks are gray or bronzy-gray, with a conspicuous whitish band on the flanks. They are white underneath. Fin tips and the back edges of the fins (except the anal fin) are black. These black areas are small but very evident, and it is these that give the shark its name.

Teeth shape: The upper teeth have one cusp, are quite narrow, pointed, and slightly oblique, with finely serrated edges. The lower teeth are very similar, but are smaller than the uppers.

(Alberto Gallucci)

Dental formula: 14–15 : 1–3 : 14–15 / 13–15 : 1–2 : 13–15

Diet: Bony fish, elasmobranchs, cephalopods, crustaceans, carcasses

Habitat: Pelagic, on continental and insular shelves at depths ranging from the surface to at least 328.1 ft. Pregnant females give birth close to shore, where juveniles often remain.

Behavior: Blacktips are active and fast. They can leap out of the water and spin up to three times before dropping back into the sea. They may be found alone or in small to large groups. They are migratory and segregate by size and sex. They may approach divers closely, often without showing any aggressive behavior. Blacktips swim into schools of small fish with their mouths wide open, swallowing any fish that are inadvertently caught in their mouths.

Threat to humans: Dangerous

Notes: Blacktip sharks are rare in those New England waters where they have been seen.

Oceanic Whitetip Shark

Carcharhinus longimanus (Poey, 1861)

Order:	*Carcharhiniformes*
Family:	*Carcharhinidae*
Genus:	*Carcharhinus*
Maximum size:	*13.0 ft*
Size at birth:	*23.6–27.6 in*
Average size at maturity:	*Male: 5.7–6.5 ft*
	Female: 5.9–6.6 ft
Embryonic development:	*Placental viviparous*
Gestation:	*12 months*
Litter size:	*1–15*
Maximum age:	*16 years or more*
Distribution (area):	*New England*
Distribution (world):	*Atlantic, Pacific, and Indian Oceans*

Oceanic whitetip shark: a) lateral view, b) ventral view of the head, c) ventral view of the pectoral fin, d) upper and lower teeth, e) placoid scale.

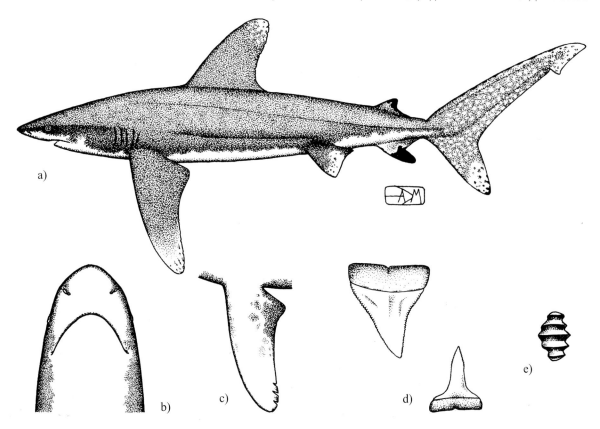

Morphology: The snouts of oceanic whitetips are relatively long and flattened, and slighty rounded in the front. The interdorsal ridge is low or absent. The first dorsal fin is very large and tall and somewhat rounded. The second dorsal fin is small, the anal fin is larger than the second dorsal fin and is long, with a deeply concave back edge. The pectoral fins are very long and wide, with slightly rounded tips. The caudal fin has a relatively long lower lobe and a very long upper lobe with a medium-size terminal lobe. Whitetips have wide mouths and short labial folds. Their eyes and nostrils are relatively small, and whitetips lack spiracles. There are five pairs of short gill slits, the last two located above the pectoral fin.

Coloration: The dorsal surfaces of whitetips are bronzy-gray, and their undersides are white. The tips of the first dorsal, pectoral, pelvic, and caudal fins have a conspicuous and irregular white patch, which gives the shark its name. The tips of the second dorsal and anal fins have a conspicuous and irregular black patch. There are additional black marks scattered on the tips of other fins. The boundary line separating the dorsal and ventral coloration is sharp and indented. The underside of the pectoral fins is white, except at the base, rear tip, and rear edge, which have the dark coloration of the dorsal surface.

(Claudio Perotti)

Teeth shape: The upper teeth have one cusp and are large, triangular, with strongly serrated edges. The lower teeth have one cusp, as well, but are smaller, narrow, pointed, erect, and with very finely serrated edges in the upper part.

Dental formula: 14–15 : 1–2 : 14–15 / 13–15 : 1 : 13–15

Diet: Bony fish, stingrays, cephalopods, marine turtles, cetaceans, gastropods, crustaceans, carcasses

Habitat: Pelagic, on continental and insular shelves, upper slopes, and ocean basins at depths ranging from the surface to at least 498.7 ft.

Behavior: Whitetips are active sharks, but usually slow swimming, though they are able to put on bursts of speed. They are equally diurnal and nocturnal and may be found alone or in groups around a food source. In groups they segregate by size and sex. They may approach divers closely, often without showing any aggressive behavior. Whitetips feed by swimming with their mouths opened wide through near-surface schooling fish as these smaller fish are being exploited by other predators, such as tuna and mackerel. When those predators leap from the sea in pursuit of small prey, they may jump straight into the wide-open mouth of the feeding oceanic whitetip. Oceanic whitetips also occasionally ingest inedible items. The conspicuous white spots at the fin tips might act as lures to attract fast-swimming prey, such as marlin, as the white spots may appear to be a school of small fish at the limit of visibility. When the prey approaches, the shark quickly accelerates and captures it. Oceanic whitetips are often accompanied by pilot fish and perhaps their presence helps to increase the visual effect, attracting prey into the shark's strike zone.

Threat to humans: Highly dangerous

Notes: Oceanic whitetip sharks are uncommon in New England waters.

Dusky Shark
Carcharhinus obscurus (LeSueur, 1818)

Order:	*Carcharhiniformes*
Family:	*Carcharhinidae*
Genus:	*Carcharhinus*
Maximum size:	*13.1 ft*
Size at birth:	*2.5–3.3 ft*
Average size at maturity:	*Male: 9.2 ft*
	Female: 8.4–9.8 ft
Embryonic development:	*Placental viviparous*
Gestation:	*Either 8–9 or 16 months*
Litter size:	*3–14*
Maximum age:	*45 years or more*
Distribution (area):	*Southern New England and Georges Bank*
Distribution (world):	*Atlantic, Pacific, and Indian Oceans*

Dusky shark: a) lateral view, b) ventral view of the head, c) ventral view of the pectoral fin, d) upper and lower teeth, e) placoid scale.

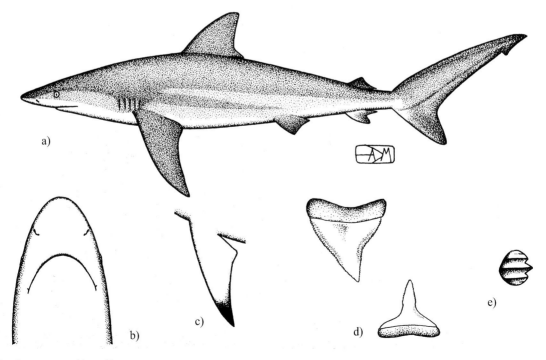

a)

b)

c)

d)

e)

Morphology: Dusky sharks have long, flattened snouts that are somewhat rounded in the front. The first dorsal fin is relatively large, as is the second, though it is still much smaller than the first dorsal. There is a low interdorsal ridge. The anal fin is about as large as the second dorsal fin and it is deeply concave. The pectoral fins are moderately long. The caudal fin has a relatively short lower lobe and a long upper lobe with a medium-size terminal lobe. The mouth is wide, with short labial folds and is parabolic when seen from below. Both the eyes and the nostrils are relatively small, and there are no spiracles. There are five pairs of short gill slits, the last two located over the base of the pectoral fin.

Coloration: Dusky sharks are dark gray-brown with a slightly bluish tint and an inconspicuous whitish band on the flanks. They are white underneath. Sometimes the fin tips are dark, and this is more evident on the anal fin. The pectoral fins are white underneath and have a black patch with faded margins at the tips and back edges.

Teeth shape: The upper teeth have one cusp, and are large, triangular, and erect to oblique, with serrated edges. The lower teeth have one cusp and are smaller, narrow, pointed, and erect to oblique, with very finely serrated edges.

Dental formula: 14–15 : 1–3 : 14–15 / 14–15 : 1–3 : 14–15

Diet: Bony fish, elasmobranchs, crustaceans, cephalopods, cetaceans, bryozoans, barnacles, carcasses

Habitat: Pelagic, on continental and insular shelves and ocean basins at depths ranging from the surface to at least 1,312.3 ft. Pregnant females give birth close inshore, where the juveniles often remain.

Behavior: Dusky sharks are active and fast. They are generally solitary, but may be found in groups. They are migratory and segregate by size. They may approach divers closely, usually without showing any aggressive behavior, and they have been known to consume inedible items.

Juvenile dusky shark.
(Alex Muench)

Threat to humans: Dangerous

Notes: Dusky sharks are rare in the New England waters where they have been reported. Harvesting this species is not permitted.

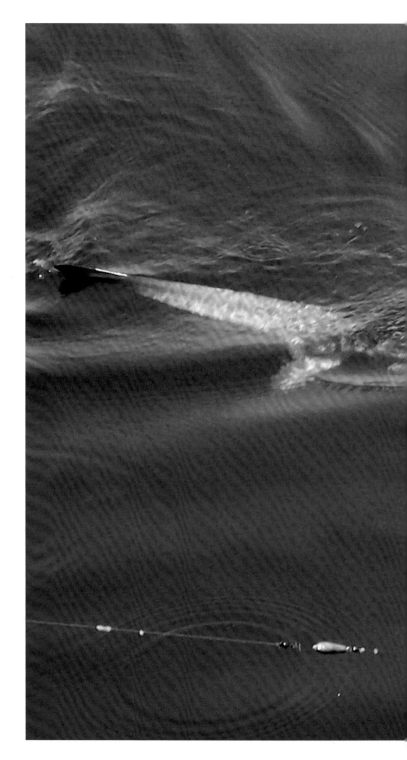

Sandbar Shark
Carcharhinus plumbeus (Poey, 1876)

Order:	*Carcharhiniformes*
Family:	*Carcharhinidae*
Genus:	*Carcharhinus*
Maximum size:	*8.2 ft*
Size at birth:	*1.8–2.5 ft*
Average size at maturity:	*Male: 4.3 ft*
	Female: 4.8 ft
Embryonic development:	*Placental viviparous*
Gestation:	*9-12 months*
Litter size:	*1-14, up to 18*
Maximum age:	*30 years, up to 50 years*
Distribution (area):	*Southern New England*
Distribution (world):	*Atlantic, Pacific, and Indian Oceans*

Sandbar shark: a) lateral view, b) ventral view of the head, c) ventral view of the pectoral fin, d) upper and lower teeth, e) placoid scale.

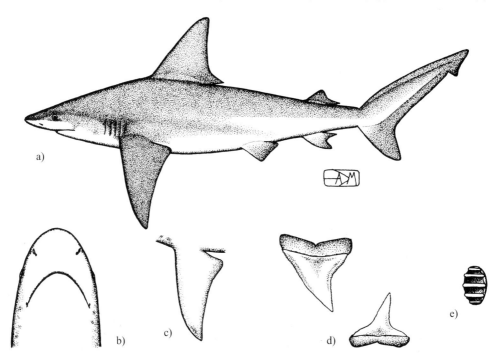

Morphology: Sandbar sharks have stout bodies with a pronounced dorsal area. The snout is short and flattened. The first dorsal fin is quite large and usually very tall, while the second dorsal fin is relatively small. There is a low interdorsal ridge connecting the two. The anal fin is about as large as the second dorsal fin and is deeply concave. The pectoral fins are long and wide, and the caudal fin has a relatively short lower lobe and a long upper lobe with a medium-size terminal lobe. The mouth is wide and curved, with short labial folds. Both the eyes and nostrils are relatively small, and there are no spiracles. There are five pairs of short gill slits, the last two located above the pectoral fin.

Coloration: Sandbar sharks are gray-brown and have an inconspicuous white band on their flanks. They are white underneath, and the tips and edges of the underside of the pectoral fins are dark.

Teeth shape: The upper teeth have one cusp and are large, triangular, and erect to oblique, with serrated edges. The lower teeth also have one cusp, but are smaller, narrow, pointed, and erect to oblique, with very finely serrated edges in the upper part and cutting edges in the lower part.

Dental formula: 14–16 : 2 : 14–16 / 12–15 : 1 : 12–15

Diet: Bony fish, elasmobranchs, molluscs, crustaceans.

(Srinayan Puppala)

Habitat: Pelagic, on continental and insular shelves and upper slopes at depths ranging from the surface to at least 1,033.5 ft. Pregnant females give birth close inshore, where newborns remain.

Behavior: Sandbar sharks are primarily nocturnal and are active and fast. They are timid and solitary, but may be seen in groups, in which they segregate by size and sex. During mating, the male bites the female in the back until she swims upside down, then he mates using both claspers.

Threat to humans: Potentially dangerous

Notes: Sandbar sharks are uncommon in those New England waters where they've been reported. Harvest of this species is prohibited.

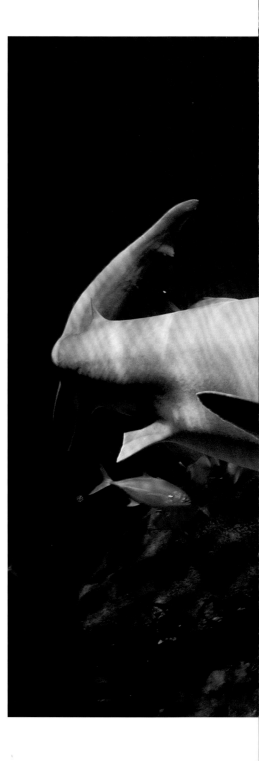

Tiger Shark

Galeocerdo cuvier (Peron & LeSueur, 1822)

Order:	*Carcharhiniformes*
Family:	*Carcharhinidae*
Genus:	*Galeocerdo*
Maximum size:	*24.3–29.9 ft*
Size at birth:	*1.7–2.5 ft*
Average size at maturity:	*Male: 7.4–9.5 ft*
	Female: 8.2–11.5 ft
Embryonic development:	*Aplacental viviparous*
Gestation:	*12 months or more*
Litter size:	*10–82*
Maximum age:	*27 years or more*
Distribution (area):	*Southern New England*
Distribution (world):	*Atlantic, Pacific, and Indian Oceans*

Tiger shark: a) lateral view, b) ventral view of the head, c) ventral view of the pectoral fin, d) upper and lower teeth, e) placoid scale.

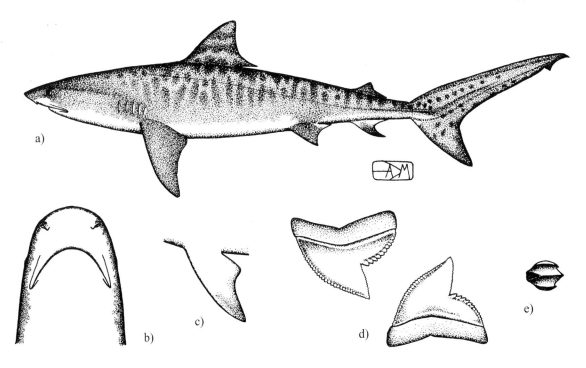

Morphology: Tiger sharks are quite massive in the front end of their bodies, but relatively slender toward the back. The snout is short, flattened, and nearly straight along the front. The first dorsal fin is relatively large, and there is an interdorsal ridge connecting it to the small second dorsal fin. The falcate (sickle-shaped) anal fin is larger than second dorsal fin and deeply concave. The pelvic fins are also falcate, and the pectoral fins are relatively short. The caudal fin has a relatively short lower lobe and a long, narrow upper lobe with a medium-size terminal lobe. There are also small caudal keels. The mouth is very wide and curved when seen from beneath. The upper labial folds are very long. The eyes are relatively small, the nostrils are moderately large, and the spiracles are small. There are five pairs of short gill slits, the last two located above the base of the pectoral fin.

Coloration: Tiger sharks are dark gray-brown, with dark vertical stripes and patches that are well evident in young but faded or absent in adults. These darks bars are what give the shark its name. As with most sharks, they are white underneath and the boundary separating the dorsal and ventral coloration is sharp and indented. The underside of the pectoral fins is partially white, with a wide grayish area at the tips and the back and front edges.

(Alberto Gallucci)

Teeth shape: Both the upper and lower teeth are large, with one cusp and a large notch on the side having strongly serrated edges (the large serrations are secondarily serrated).

Dental formula: 9–13 : 1 : 8–13 / 9–13 : 1 : 9–13

Diet: Bony fish, elasmobranchs, marine mammals, marine reptiles, cephalopods, gastropods, crustaceans, birds, tunicates, jellyfish, carcasses

Habitat: Pelagic, on continental and insular shelves and ocean basins at depths ranging from the surface to at least 1,000.6 ft. Tiger sharks live offshore during the day, but may move close inshore at night.

Behavior: Tiger sharks are active, but usually slow swimming, though they are able to put on bursts of speed. They are primarily nocturnal and solitary, but may be found in small groups around a food source. They may approach divers closely, often without showing any aggressive behavior. Tiger sharks are well known for their indiscriminate diet and will frequently ingest inedible items.

Threat to humans: Highly dangerous

Notes: Along with bull and great white sharks, tiger sharks are among the three species most likely to attack humans. They are very rare in New England waters.

Blue Shark

Prionace glauca (Linnaeus, 1758)

Order:	*Carcharhiniformes*
Family:	*Carcharhinidae*
Genus:	*Prionace*
Maximum size:	*12.6 ft*
Size at birth:	*1.2–1.7 ft*
Average size at maturity:	*Male: 5.7–9.2 ft*
	Female: 4.8–7.3 ft
Embryonic development:	*Placental viviparous*
Gestation:	*9–12 months*
Litter size:	*3–135*
Maximum age:	*20 years or more*
Distribution (area):	*New England*
Distribution (world):	*Atlantic, Pacific, and Indian Oceans*

Blue shark: a) lateral view, b) ventral view of the head, c) ventral view of the pectoral fin, d) upper and lower teeth, e) placoid scale.

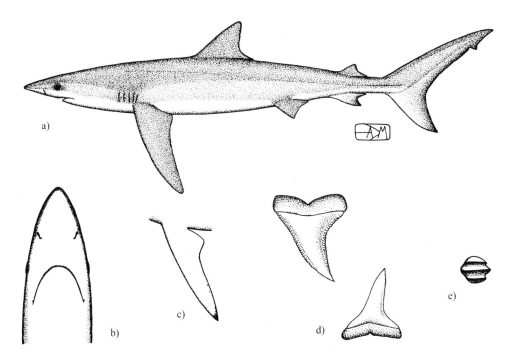

Morphology: Blue sharks have slender bodies with a long, narrow snout. The first dorsal fin is relatively large, and is located well behind the pectoral fins, which are very long and narrow. The second dorsal fin is small, and the anal fin is about as large as the second dorsal fin. The caudal fin has a moderately long lower lobe and a much longer upper lobe, with a large terminal lobe. There are small caudal keels. The mouth is wide and parabolic when viewed from below, and the labial folds are short. The eyes are quite large, the nostrils are small, and there are no spiracles. There are five pairs of short gill slits, the last two located over the pectoral fin.

Coloration: This species gets its name from its bright blue dorsal coloring, though, like most sharks, it is white underneath. The tips and the back edges of the fins have a narrow, inconspicuous black band. These black colorings also appear on the underside of the pectoral fins.

Teeth shape: The upper teeth have one cusp and are large, long, relatively narrow, curved, oblique, and with strongly serrated edges. The lower teeth are similar, but are narrower, with edges finely serrated in the upper part and smooth at the base.

(Joe Romeiro)

Dental formula: 13–16 : 1–2 : 13–16 / 13–16 : 1–4 : 13–16

Diet: Molluscs, bony fish and their eggs, sharks, crustaceans, cetaceans, nematodes, birds, carcasses

Habitat: Pelagic, on continental and insular shelves and ocean basins at depths ranging from the surface to at least 2,001.3 ft. Blue sharks live offshore during the day, but may move close inshore at night. Pregnant females give birth in shallow water.

Behavior: Blue sharks are active and fast, and primarily nocturnal. They are generally solitary, but can be found in huge numbers around a source of food. They are migratory and segregate by sex and size. Blue sharks may approach divers closely, and generally do so without showing any aggressive behavior. They feed on schooling fish and squid by taking bites from the tightly massed prey or swimming through the school with their mouths wide open, ingesting any prey that inadvertently run into their jaws.

Threat to humans: Dangerous

Notes: Blue sharks are common in southern New England waters. They are regular summer visitors to the southern and western parts of the Gulf of Maine, appearing occasionally in July, but more often in August and September. They are common on Georges Bank in the summer. This population of blue sharks is known to migrate from New England waters to northeastern South America and across the Atlantic Ocean. They are commonly caught by both commercial and sport fishermen. Cage diving to observe blue sharks is done in the ocean off Rhode Island.

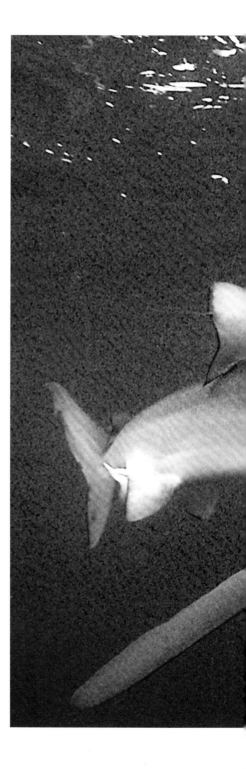

(Walter Heim)

Atlantic Sharpnose Shark
Rhizoprionodon terraenovae (Richardson, 1836)

Order:	*Carcharhiniformes*
Family:	*Carcharhinidae*
Genus:	*Rhizoprionodon*
Maximum size:	*3.6 ft*
Size at birth:	*11.4–14.6 ft*
Average size at maturity:	*Male: 2.1–2.6 ft*
	Female: 2.8–3.0 ft
Embryonic development:	*Placental viviparous*
Gestation:	*10–11 months*
Litter size:	*1–7*
Maximum age:	*Unknown*
Distribution (area):	*New England*
Distribution (world):	*Western Atlantic Ocean*

Atlantic sharpnose shark: a) lateral view, b) ventral view of the head, c) ventral view of the pectoral fin, d) upper and lower teeth, e) placoid scale.

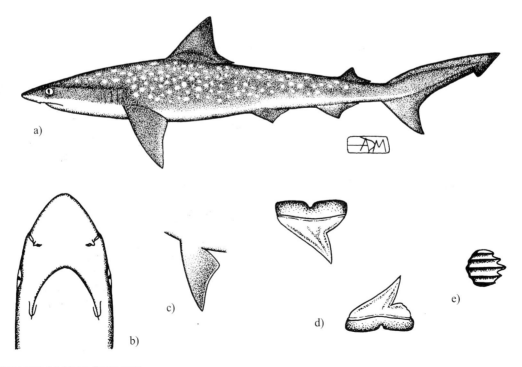

Morphology: Atlantic sharpnose sharks are relatively small sharks, with a long, flattened snout. The first dorsal fin is relatively large, and the second is small. The interdorsal ridge is either quite low or may be absent. The anal fin is slightly smaller than the second dorsal fin and there are long preanal ridges (a pair of ridges extending back from the anal fin along the caudal peduncle). Pectoral fins are short. The caudal fin has a relatively short lower lobe and a much longer upper lobe with a large terminal lobe. The mouth is wide and curved when seen from below, and the labial folds are relatively short. The eyes are large, the nostrils are relatively small, and there are no spiracles. The last two pairs of the five gill slit pairs are located over the pectoral fin.

Coloration: Atlantic sharpnose sharks are gray to gray-brown in color and, like most sharks, white underneath. Large specimens have small light spots. The pectoral fins have white posterior edges, and the dorsal and caudal fins have dusky colored tips and posterior edges.

Teeth shape: Both the upper and lower teeth have one cusp, and are large, oblique, with a large notch on the lateral margin, and with finely serrated edges. Lower teeth are similar to uppers. In juveniles, teeth lack serrated edges.

Dental formula: 11–13 : 11–13 / 12–13 :12–13

Diet: Bony fish, crustaceans, worms, molluscs

Habitat: Pelagic, on continental shelves at depths ranging from the surface to at least 918.6 ft. Females give birth in shallow water.

Behavior: Migratory

Threat to humans: Not dangerous

Notes: Atlantic sharpnose sharks are not common in New England.

(Mark Sampson)

Bonnethead Shark

Sphyrna tiburo (Linnaeus, 1758)

Order:	*Carcharhiniformes*
Family:	*Sphyrnidae*
Genus:	*Sphyrna*
Maximum size:	*4.9 ft*
Size at birth:	*1.2–1.3 ft*
Average size at maturity:	*Male: 1.7–2.5 ft*
	Female: 2.8 ft
Embryonic development:	*Placental viviparous*
Gestation:	*Unknown*
Litter size:	*4–16*
Maximum age:	*12 years or more*
Distribution (area):	*Connecticut and Rhode Island*
Distribution (world):	*Western Atlantic and Eastern Pacific Oceans*

Bonnethead shark: a) lateral view, b) ventral view of the head,
c) ventral view of the pectoral fin, d) upper and lower teeth

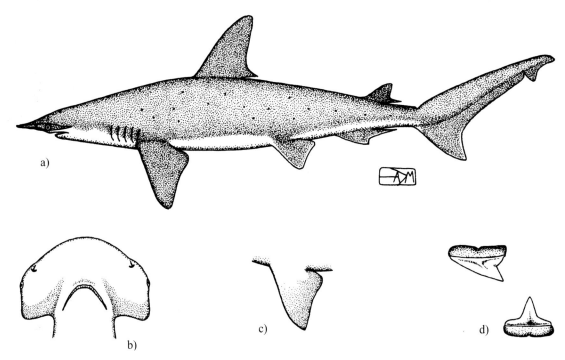

Morphology: Bonnethead sharks are the smallest member of the hammerhead shark family. The head is greatly flattened and moderately expanded sideways, resembling a moderately large hammer. The front edge of the head is curved, while the back edge is slightly concave. The fins are not falcate or hooked. The first dorsal fin is large and tall, while the second dorsal fin is small. The base of the anal fin is much longer than the base of the second dorsal fin. Both the pelvic and the pectoral fins are short. The caudal fin has a relatively short lower lobe and a long upper lobe with a medium-size terminal lobe. The mouth is wide, with short labial folds, and it is parabolic when seen from underneath. The eyes are small and located on the outside edges of the expanded head, the nostrils are long, and there are no spiracles. There are five pairs of short gill slits, the last two located above the base of the pectoral fin.

Coloration: Bonnethead sharks are gray or gray-brown to grayish-green on their dorsal surfaces, often with small dark patches. They are whitish underneath. The underside of the pectoral fins are light grayish fading to white toward the base.

Teeth shape: The upper teeth have one cusp and are oblique with cutting edges. The lower teeth also have one cusp and are smaller, pointed, and erect. The exception to this is the posterior teeth, which lack the cusp and are relatively large, resembling molars.

(Tennessee Aquarium / Todd Stailey)

Dental formula: 12–14 : 0–1 : 12–14 / 12–14 : 1 : 12–14

Diet: Crustaceans, molluscs, bony fish

Habitat: Pelagic, on continental and insular shelves at depths ranging from the surface to at least 262.5 ft. Females give birth in shallow water.

Behavior: Bonnethead sharks are solitary, but may be seen in groups as large as 700 sharks. They are migratory, segregate by sex, and seem to communicate with each other through a complex body language. This species is able to reproduce by parthenogenesis—the direct development of an embryo from an egg without male genetic contribution.

Threat to humans: Potentially dangerous

Notes: Bonnethead sharks are very rare in the New England waters they've been encountered.

Smooth Hammerhead

Sphyrna zygaena (Linnaeus, 1758)

Order:	*Carcharhiniformes*
Family:	*Sphyrnidae*
Genus:	*Sphyrna*
Maximum size:	*12.1–13.1 ft*
Size at birth:	*1.5–2.0 ft*
Average size at maturity:	*Male: 6.9–8.2 ft*
	Female: 6.9–8.7 ft
Embryonic development:	*Placental viviparous*
Gestation:	*Unknown*
Litter size:	*29–37*
Maximum age:	*Unknown*
Distribution (area):	*New England*
Distribution (world):	*Atlantic, Pacific, and Indian Oceans*

Smooth hammerhead: a) lateral view, b) ventral view of the head, c) ventral view of the pectoral fin, d) upper and lower teeth

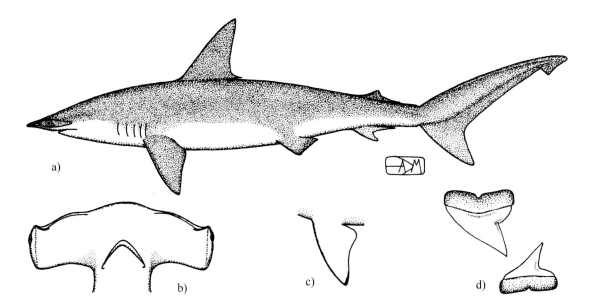

Morphology: Smooth hammerhead sharks have a very distinctive appearance. The head is greatly flattened and greatly expanded sideways, resembling a large hammer. The fins are not falcate or hooked. The first dorsal fin is large and tall, the second dorsal fin is small. The anal fin is about as large as the second dorsal fin. The pelvic and pectoral fins are short. The caudal fin has a relatively short lower lobe and a long upper lobe with a medium-size terminal lobe. The mouth is wide and parabolic when viewed from below, and the labial folds are short. The eyes are small and set far apart at each side of the head. The nostrils are long, and there are no spiracles. There are five pairs of short gill slits, the last two located above the base of the pectoral fin.

Coloration: Smooth hammerheads are olive brown or gray-brown on their dorsal surfaces and white underneath. The undersides of the pectoral fins have small black patches at the tips.

Teeth shape: The upper teeth have one cusp and are oblique, with cutting edges, except on the tooth sides near the base, which have finely serrated edges. The lower teeth have one cusp and are smaller, pointed, and oblique.

Dental formula: 14–15 : 1–2 : 14–15 / 14 : 1 : 14.

Diet: Bony fish, elasmobranchs, cetaceans, crustaceans, molluscs, carcasses

Habitat: Pelagic, on continental and insular shelves, upper slopes, and ocean basins at depths ranging from the surface to at least 328.1 ft. Females give birth close inshore, where juveniles often remain, while males stay in deeper waters.

(Sabine Wintner / Natal Sharks Board)

Behavior: Smooth hammerhead sharks are active, but rather timid. They are migratory and may be found alone or in groups, some of which can be very large—up to 1,200 specimens—in which they segregate by size. These sharks have a greater number of ampullae of Lorenzini on the underside of their wide head. They likely use their head to find and scoop hidden animals from the sand. They also use their uniquely shaped head to pin prey against the sea bottom while maneuvering their body to grasp the prey in their mouth. Their head shape also allows for improved hydrodynamics, increased sensitivity to vibrations in the water, the ability to better follow odor traces, and improved depth perception.

Threat to humans: Potentially dangerous

Notes: In the summer, smooth hammerheads often wander in small groups north to southern New England waters, but they rarely venture north of Cape Cod.

R eporting the capture or sighting of sharks is of great value to shark researchers. Anyone can help in the ongoing research of sharks in New England waters. Any data collected with your help will be archived for future studies. Note that information on all shark species is considered interesting, not just data concerning the larger species.

To help with this data collection, an outline of the desired information and an address to send it is provided below. Please provide information as accurately and completely as possible. However, even incomplete information is still of great value and should be submitted. If you go sport-fishing and catch sharks, we strongly recommend that the animal be set free after capture. We also encourage the tagging of sharks, which can be very rewarding. Most shark populations are in alarming decline, and this is one way you can contribute to the conservation of these wonderful animals. For released sharks, it is not essential that all the data be supplied.

In order to make your contribution as useful as possible, measure the total length of the shark in a straight line, from the tip of the snout to the tip of the upper lobe of the caudal fin. If it is not possible to accurately measure the specimen, specify that the reported measure is an estimate.

The weight is considered less important, but if available, should be taken on the whole specimen. If the whole weight cannot be determined, specify if the specimen has been gutted, beheaded, de-finned, or other. As with the length, specify that the reported weight is an estimate if the shark was not actually weighed.

The sex of the specimen can be easily determined by observing the underside of the shark near the pelvic fins (the pair of fins located in the pelvic region). Males have two claspers (copulatory organs) in the shape of cylindrical appendages.

If possible, take a photo of the shark. It will be very useful, both for allowing an expert to identify the species and as a record for the archives. Take the picture of the whole specimen from its side. Additional photos of details, especially the underside of the head and the teeth, are also very valuable.

We thank you in advance for your participation.

Reporting Information:

Species

Type of encounter (capture, underwater, sighting, attack), date, and time

Location (GPS or latitude/longitude), depth, and distance from shore

Weather and marine conditions

Length and weight

Sex

Stomach contents (if caught)

Behavior

Presence of other animals in the immediate area

Other details and comments

Submit this information to:

Apex Predators Program
NOAA/National Marine Fisheries Service
28 Tarzwell Drive
Narragansett, RI 02882

Block Island, Rhode Island. On August 5, 1983, a 15.9-ft. TL male great white shark was caught in these waters.
(Gary E. Eddey, Matheny School and Hospital / courtesy of NOAA Photo Library)

Sandbar sharks and sand tiger sharks in the Open Ocean Exhibit of the Maritime
Aquarium at Norwalk, Connecticut.
(The Maritime Aquarium at Norwalk, Connecticut)

ACUÑA, E. & J.C. VILLAROEL (2003): Distribution, abundance, and reproductive biology of the blue shark *Prionace glauca* in the Southeastern Pacific Ocean. *AES Abstracts Manaus, Brazil, June 27–June 30*: 36.

BARRULL, J. & I. MATE (2002): *Tiburones del Mediterráneo.* Llibreria El Set-ciències, Arenys de Mar, 292 pp.

BASS, A.J., D'AUBREY, J.D. & N. KISTNASAMY (1973–1976): Sharks of the east coast of Southern Africa. 1–6, *Investigational Report of the Oceanographic Research Institute, Durban,* 33, 37, 38, 39, 43, 45.

BAUCHOT, M.L. (1987): Requins. Pp. 767–843 in: Fischer W., Schneider M. & M.-L. Bauchot (eds.): *Fiches FAO d'identification des espèces pour les besoins de la pêche. (Révision l). Méditerranée et Mer Noire. Zone de pêche 37. Vol. 2. Vertébrés.* Rome, CEE, FAO.

BENZ, G.W., J.D. BORUCINSKA, L.F. LOWRY, H.E. WHITELEY, (2002): Ocular lesions associated with attachment of the copepod *Ommatokoita elongata* (Lernaeopodidae: Siphonostomatoida) to corneas of Pacific sleeper sharks *Somniosus pacificus* captured off Alaska in Prince William Sound. *The Journal of Parasitology,* 88(3): 474–481.

BENZ, G.W., Z. LUCAS, L.F. LOWRY, (1998): New Host and Ocean Records for the Copepod, *Ommatokoita elongata* (Siphonostomatoida: Lernaeopodidae), a Parasite of the Eyes of Sleeper Sharks. *The Journal of Parasitology,* 84(6): 1271–1274.

BIGELOW, H.B. & W.C. SCHROEDER (1948): Sharks. Pp. 53–576 in: *Fishes of the Western North Atlantic. Part one: Lancelets, Ciclostomes, Sharks.* Memoir Sears Foundation for Marine Research, Yale University.

BIGELOW, H.B. & W.C. SCHROEDER (1953): *Fishes of the Gulf of Maine.* Fishery Bulletin, 74(53): 577 pp.

BIGELOW, H.B. & W.C. SCHROEDER (1957): A study of the sharks of the suborder *Squaloidea. Bulletin of the Museum of Comparative Zoology, Harvard University,* 117(1): 1–150.

BORUCINSKA, J.D., G.W. BENZ, & H.E. WHITELEY (1998): Ocular lesions associated with attachment of the parasitic copepod *Ommatokoita elongata* (Grant), to corneas of Greenland sharks, *Somniosus microcephalus* (Bloch and Schneider). *Journal of Fish Diseases,* 21 (6): 415.

BUENCUERPO, V., S. RIOS, J. MORON, (1998): Pelagic sharks associated with the swordfish, *Xiphias gladius,* fishery in the eastern North Atlantic Ocean and the Strait of Gibraltar. *Fishery Bulletin,* 96(4): 667–685.

CADENAT, J. & J. BLACHE (1981): Requins de Méditerranée et d'Atlantique (plus particulièrement de la Côte Occidentale d'Afrique). *Faune Tropicale, ORSTOM, Paris,* 21: 1–330.

CAPAPÉ, C. (1974): Observation sur la sexualité, la reproduction et la fécundité de 8 Séléciens pleurotrêmes vivipares placentaires des côtes tunisiennes. *Archives de l'Institut Pasteur de Tunis,* 51(4): 329-344.

CAPAPÉ, C. (1975): Observations sur le régime alimentaire de 29 Selaciens pleurotêrmes des côtes tunisiennes. *Archives de l'Institut Pasteur de Tunis,* 52(4): 395–414.

CAPAPÉ, C. (1989): Les Sélaciens des côtes méditerranéennes: aspects generaux de leur écologie et exemples de peuplements. *Océanis,* 15 (3): 309–331.

CARLSON, J.K. & G.R. PARSONS (1997): Age and growth of the bonnethead shark, *Sphyrna tiburo,* from northwest Florida, with comments on clinal variation. *Environmental Biology of Fishes,* 50(3): 331–341.

CASTRO, J. (1983): *The Sharks of North American Waters.* Texas A&M University Press, College Station, 180 pp.

CELONA, A., N. DONATO & A. DE MADDALENA (2001): In relation to the captures of a great white shark *Carcharodon carcharias* (Linnaeus, 1758) and a shortfin mako, *Isurus oxyrinchus* (Rafinesque, 1809), in the Messina Strait. *Annales, Series historia naturalis,* 11(1): 13–16.

CELONA, A., PISCITELLI, L. & A. DE MADDALENA (2004): Two large shortfin makos, *Isurus oxyrinchus* (Rafinesque, 1809) caught off Sicily, Western Ionian Sea. *Annales, Series historia naturalis,* 14(1): 35–42.

CLIFF, G., L.J.V. COMPAGNO, M.J. SMALE, R.P. VAN DER ELST, & S.P. WINTNER (2000): First records of white sharks, *Carcharodon carcharias,* from Mauritius, Zanzibar, Madagascar and Kenya. *South African Journal of Science,* 96. 365–367.

CLIFF, G., S.F.J. DUDLEY, & B. DAVIS (1989): Sharks caught in the protective gill nets off Natal, South Africa. 2. The great white shark, *Carcharodon carcharias* (Linnaeus). *South African Journal of Marine Science,* 8: 131–144.

CLIFF, G., S.F.J. DUDLEY, & B. DAVIS (1989): Sharks caught in the protective gill nets off Natal, South Africa. 3. The shortfin mako shark, *Isurus oxyrinchus* (Linnaeus). *South African Journal of Marine Science,* 9: 115–126.

COLLIER, R.S. (2003): *Shark Attacks of the Twentieth Century from the Pacific Coast of North America.* Scientia Publishing, LLC, Chatsworth, 296 pp.

COLLIER, R.S., M. MARKS, & R.W. WARNER (1996): White shark attacks on inanimate objects along the Pacific coast of North America. Pp. 217–221 in: Klimley, A.P. & D.G. Ainley (eds.) *Great white sharks: The biology of* Carcharodon carcharias. Academic Press, San Diego, 518 pp.

COMPAGNO, L.J.V. (1984): FAO Species Catalogue. Vol.4. *Sharks of the World. An annotated and illustrated catalogue of sharks species known to date. Parts 1 and 2.* FAO Fisheries Synopsis, 125: 1–655.

COMPAGNO, L.J.V. (2001): *Sharks of the World. An annotated and illustrated catalogue of shark species known to date. Volume 2. Bullhead, mackerel and carpet sharks (Heterodontiformes, Lamniformes and Orectolobiformes).* FAO Species Catalogue for Fishery Purposes. No. 1, Vol. 2. FAO, Rome, 269 pp.

COMPAGNO, L.J.V., M. DANDO, & S. FOWLER (2005): *Sharks of the world.* Princeton University Press, Princeton, 368 pp.

COUSTEAU, J.P. & P. COUSTEAU (1970): *The Shark: Splendid Savage of the Sea.* Cassell, London, 277 pp.

DE LA SERNA, J. M., J. VALEIRAS, J. M. ORTIZ, & D. MACIAS (2002): Large pelagic sharks as by-catch in the Mediterranean swordfish longline fishery: some biological aspects. *Northwest Atlantic Fisheries Organization, Scientific Council Meeting –*

September 2002: 1–33.

DE MADDALENA, A. (2000c): Il disegno della superficie ventrale delle pinne pettorali dei Selaci come carattere diagnostico per il riconoscimento delle specie. *Annales, Series historia naturalis*, 10(2): 187–198.

DE MADDALENA, A. (2002a): *Lo squalo bianco nei mari d'Italia*. Ireco, Formello, 144 pp.

DE MADDALENA, A. (2008): *Sharks - The Perfect Predators*. Jacana Media, Houghton, 198 pp.

DE MADDALENA, A. & H. BAENSCH (2005): *Haie im Mittelmeer*. Franckh-Kosmos Verlags-GmbH & Co., Stuttgart, 240 pp.

DE MADDALENA, A. & A. "THE SHARKMAN" BUTTIGIEG (2009): *Pesci martello - Hammerhead sharks*. Edizioni Ireco, Formello, 128 pp.

DE MADDALENA, A., O. GLAIZOT, & G. OLIVER (2003): On the great white shark, *Carcharodon carcharias* (Linnaeus, 1758), preserved in the Museum of Zoology in Lausanne. *Marine Life*, 13(1/2): 53–59.

DE MADDALENA, A. & W. HEIM (2009): *Great White Sharks in United States Museums*. McFarland, Jefferson NC.

DE MADDALENA, A., A. PRETI, & R. SMITH (2005): *Mako sharks*. Krieger Publishing, Malabar, 72 pp.

DE MADDALENA, A., M. ZUFFA, L. LIPEJ & A. CELONA (2001): An analysis of the photographic evidences of the largest great white sharks, *Carcharodon carcharias* (Linnaeus, 1758), captured in the Mediterranean Sea with considerations about the maximum size of the species. *Annales, Series historia naturalis*, 11(2): 193–206.

DIODATI, P. (2004): Scientists and fishermen team up to move white shark final 100 yards to open water. *Marine Fisheries Advisory*, October 6, 2004.

EBERT, D.A. (2003): *Sharks, Rays and Chimaeras of California*. University of California Press, Berkeley and Los Angeles, 286 pp.

EBERT, D.A., L.J.V. COMPAGNO, & P.D. COWLEY. (1992): A preliminary investigation of the feeding ecology of squaloid sharks off the west coast of southern Africa. *South African Journal of Marine Science*, 12: 601–609.

ELLIS, R. (1983): *The Book of Sharks*. Robert Hale, London, 256 pp.

ELLIS, R. & J.E. McCOSKER (1991): *Great White Shark*. Stanford University Press, Stanford, 270 pp.

FRANCIS, M.P. (1996): Observations on a pregnant white shark with a review of reproductive biology. Pp. 157–172 in: Klimley, A.P. & D.G. Ainley (eds) *Great white sharks: The biology of* Carcharodon carcharias. Academic Press, San Diego, 518 pp.

FROESE, R. & D. PAULY (Eds) (2006): *FishBase*. World Wide Web electronic publication. www.fishbase.org, version (02/2006).

GARRICK, J.A.F (1967): Revision of sharks of genus *Isurus* with description of a new species (Galeoidea, Lamnidae). *Proceedings of the United States National Museum*, 118: 663–690.

GARRICK, J.A.F (1982): Sharks of the genus *Carcharhinus*. *NOAA Technical Report NMFS Circular*, 445: 1–194.

GOLDMAN, K.J., S.D. ANDERSON, J.E. McCOSKER, & A.P. KLIMLEY (1996): Temperature, swimming depth, and movements of a white shark at the South Farallon Islands, California. Pp. 111-120 in: Klimley, A.P. & D.G. Ainley (eds.) *Great*

White Sharks: The Biology of Carcharodon carcharias. Academic Press, San Diego, 518 pp.

GOODE, G.B. & T.H BEAN (1896): Oceanic ichthyology, a treatise on the deep-sea and pelagic fishes of the world, based chiefly upon the collections made by steamers Blake, Albatross and Fish Hawk in the northwestern Atlantic. *Smithson. Contrib. Knowl.*, 30 and *Spec. Bull U.S. natn. Mus.*, 1895 [1896] and *Mem. Mus. comp. Zool. Harv.*, 1 (Text): xxxv+1–553; 2 (Atlas): xxiii+1–26, 123 pl., 417 fig.

HANNAN, K. (2005): Determination of gastric evacuation rate for spiny dogfish, *Squalus acanthias*. First International Symposium on the Management & Biology of Dogfish Sharks. June 13–15, 2005, Seattle, Washington. Abstracts: 9.

HARTELL, K.E., C.P. KENALEY, J.K. GALBRAITH, & T.T. SUTTON (2008): Additional records of deep-sea fishes from off Greater New England. *Northeastern Naturalist*, 15(3): 317–334.

IGLÉSIAS, S.P., K. NAKAYA & M. STEHMANN (2004): *Apristurus melanoasper*, a new species of deep-water catshark from the North Atlantic (*Chondrichthyes*: *Carcharhiniformes*: *Scyliorhinidae*). *Cybium*, 28(4):345–356.

JARDAS, I. (1972): Supplement to the knowledge of ecology of some adriatic cartilaginous fishes (*Chondrichthyes*) with special reference to their nutrition. *Acta Adriatica*, 14(7): 1–60.

JOHNSON, R.H. (1978): *Sharks of Polynesia*. Les Editions du Pacifique, Papeete, 170 pp.

JONES, T.S. & K.I. UGLAND (2001): Reproduction of female spiny dogfish, *Squalus acanthias*, in the Oslofjord. *Fishery Bulletin*, 99: 685–690.

KABASAKAL, H. (2001): Preliminary data on the feeding ecology of some selachians from the north-eastern Aegean Sea. *Acta Adriatica*, 42(2): 15–24.

KABASAKAL, H. (2002a): Cephalopods in the stomach contents of four Elasmobranch species from the northern Aegean Sea. *Acta Adriatica*, 43(1): 17–24.

KLIMLEY, A.P., P. PYLE, & S.D. ANDERSON (1996): Tail slap and breach: agonistic displays among white sharks? Pp. 241-255 in: Klimley, A.P. & D.G. Ainley (eds.) *Great White Sharks: The Biology of* Carcharodon carcharias. Academic Press, San Diego, 518 pp.

KLIMLEY, A.P., B.J. LE BOEUF, K.M. CANTARA, J.E. RICHERT, S.F. DAVIS, S. VAN SOMMERAN, & J.T. KELLY (2001): The hunting strategy of white sharks, *Carcharodon carcharias*, near a seal colony. *Marine Biology*, 138: 617–636.

KOHLER, N.E., J.G. CASEY, & P.A. TURNER (1996): Length-length and length-weight relationships for 13 shark species from the Western North Atlantic. *NOAA Technical Memorandum NMFS-NE-110*: 1–22.

KOHLER, N.E., CASEY, J.G. & P.A. TURNER (1998): NMFS Cooperative Shark Tagging Program, 1962-93: an atlas of shark tag and recapture data. *Marine Fisheries Review*, 60(2): 1–87.

KOHLER, N.E., P.A. TURNER, J.J. HOEY, L.J. NATANSON, & R. BRIGGS (2002): Tag and recapture data for three pelagic shark species: blue shark, *Prionace glauca*, shortfin mako, *Isurus oxyrinchus*, and porbeagle, *Lamna nasus*, in the North Atlantic Ocean. *Col. Vol. Sci. Pap. ICCATT, 54(4)*: 1231–1260.

LAST, P.R. & J.D. STEVENS (1994): *Sharks and rays of Australia*. CSIRO, Australia, 514 pp.

LE BOEUF, B. (2004): Hunting and migratory movements of white sharks in the eastern North Pacific. *Mem. Natl. Inst. Polar*

Res., Spec. Issue, 58: 91–102.

LE BRASSEUR, R.J. (1964): Stomach Contents of Blue Shark Taken in the Gulf of Alaska. *Journal Fisheries Research Board of Canada*, 21(4): 861–862.

LINEAWEAVER, T.H. III & R.H. BACKUS (1969): *The Natural History of Sharks*. J.B. Lippincott Co., Philadelphia, 256 pp.

LIPEJ, L., A. DE MADDALENA, & A. SOLDO (2004): *Sharks of the Adriatic Sea*. Knjiznica Annales Majora, Koper, 254 pp.

LITVINOV, F.F. & V.V. LAPTIKHOVSKY (2005): Methods of investigations of shark heterodonty and dental formulae's variability with the blue shark, *Prionace glauca,* taken as an example. *ICES CM DOCUMENTS 2005*, Theme Session on Elasmobranch Fisheries Science (N): 27, International Council for the Exploration of the Sea.

LO BIANCO, S. (1909): Notizie biologiche riguardanti specialmente il periodo di maturità sessuale degli animali del Golfo di Napoli. *Mittheilungen aus der Zoologischen Station zu Neapel*, 19(4): 513–761.

LONG, D.J. & R.E. JONES (1996): White Shark predation and scavenging on Cetaceans in the Eastern North Pacific Ocean. Pp. 293–307 in Klimley, A.P. & D.G. Ainley (eds.) *Great White Sharks: The Biology of* Carcharodon carcharias. Academic Press, San Diego, 518 pp.

MARTIN, R.A. (1995): *Shark Smart: The Divers' Guide to Understanding Shark Behavior*. Diving Naturalist Press, Vancouver, 180 pp.

MARTIN, R.A. (2003): *Field Guide to the Great White Shark*. ReefQuest Centre for Shark Research, Special Publication No. 1, 192 pp.

MATTHEWS, L.H. (1962): The shark that hibernates. *New Scientist*, 280: 415–421.

McCOSKER, J.E. (1987): The white shark, *Carcharodon carcharias*, has a warm stomach. *Copeia*, 1987: 195–197.

MICHAEL, S.W. (1993): *Reef Sharks and Rays of the World*. Sea Challengers, Monterey, 107 pp.

MOLLET, H.F. & G.M. CAILLIET (1996): Using allometry to predict body mass from linear measurements of the white shark. Pp. 81–90 in: Klimley, A.P. & D.G. Ainley (eds.): *Great white sharks. The biology of* Carcharodon carcharias. Academic Press, San Diego, 518 pp.

MOLLET, H.F., G.M. CAILLIET, A.P. KLIMLEY, D.A. EBERT, A.D. TESTI, & L.J.V. COMPAGNO (1996): A review of length validation methods and protocols to measure large white sharks. Pp. 91–108 in: Klimley, A.P. & D.G. Ainley (eds.): *Great White Sharks. The Biology of* Carcharodon carcharias. Academic Press, San Diego, 518 pp.

MOLLET, H.F., G. CLIFF, H.L. PRATT, Jr. & J.D. STEVENS (2000): Reproductive biology of the female shortfin mako, *Isurus oxyrinchus* (Rafinesque, 1810), with comments on the embryonic development of lamnoids. *Fishery Bulletin*, 98: 299–318.

MOORE, J.A., K.E. HARTELL, J.E. CRADDOCK, & J.K. GALBRAITH (2003): An annotated list of deepwater fishes from off the New England region, with new area records. *Northeastern Naturalist*, 10(2): 159–248.

MORENO, J.A. (1989): Biología reproductiva y fenología de *Alopias vulpinus* (Bonnaterre, 1788) en el Atlántico Nororiental y Mediterráneo Occidental. *Scientia Marina*, 1989, 53(1): 37–46.

MORENO, J.A. (1995): *Guía de los tiburones del Atlántico Nororiental y Mediterráneo*. Ed. Pirámide, Madrid, 310 pp.

MYRBERG, A. Jr (1987): Shark behaviour. Pp. 84–92 in: Stevens, J.D. (ed.) *Sharks*. Intercontinental Publishing Corporation Limited, Hong Kong, 240 pp.

NATANSON, L.J., MELLO, J.J. & S.E. CAMPANA (2002): Validated age and growth of the porbeagle shark, *Lamna nasus*, in the western North Atlantic. *Fishery Bulletin*, 100(2): 266–278.

OFFICE OF SUSTAINABLE FISHERIES HIGHLY MIGRATORY SPECIES MANAGEMENT DIVISION (2008): *2009 Commercial Compliance Guide. Guide for Complying with the Atlantic Tunas, Swordfish, Sharks, and Billfish Regulations*. U.S. Department of Commerce, National Oceanic and Atmospheric Administration, National Marine Fisheries Service, 42 pp.

OFFICE OF SUSTAINABLE FISHERIES HIGHLY MIGRATORY SPECIES MANAGEMENT DIVISION (2008): *2009 Recreational Compliance Guide. Guide for Complying with the Atlantic Tunas, Swordfish, Sharks, and Billfish Regulations*. U.S. Department of Commerce, National Oceanic and Atmospheric Administration, National Marine Fisheries Service, 25 pp.

OLIVER, J. (2009): Fisheries of the Northeastern United States; 2009 Specifications for the Spiny Dogfish Fishery. *Federal Register*, 74(83): 20230–20234.

OVERSTROM, N.A. (1989): Estimated tooth replacement rate in captive sand tiger sharks, *Carcharias taurus* (Rafinesque, 1810). *Copeia*, 1991: 525–526.

PARKER, H.W. & M. BOESEMAN (1954): The basking shark, *Cetorhinus maximus*, in winter. *Proceedings of the Zoological Society of London*, 124(1): 185–194.

POLL, M. (1951): Poissons. 1. Generalités. 2. Sélaciens et Chimères. *Result. Sci. Exped. Oceanogr. Belge*, 4(1): 1–154.

PRATT, H.L. Jr. (1996): Reproduction in the male white shark. Pp. 131-138 in: Klimley, A.P. & D.G. Ainley (eds.): *Great white sharks. The biology of* Carcharodon carcharias. Academic Press, San Diego, 518 pp.

PRETI, A., S.E. SMITH, & D.A. RAMON (2001): Feeding habits of the common thresher shark, *Alopias vulpinus*, sampled from the California-based drift gill net fishery, 1998-99. *California Cooperative Oceanic Fisheries Investigations Reports*, 42: 145–152.

PUNZÓN, A. & M.A. HERRERA (2000): Feeding of *Centroscyllium fabricii* and the influence of discards on its diet in Flemish Pass (north-west Atlantic). *Journal of the Marine Biological Association of the United Kingdom*, 80(4): 755–756.

RANDALL, J.E. (1986): *Sharks of Arabia*. IMMEL Publishing, London, 148 pp.

RANZI, S. (1932–1934): Le basi fisio-morfologiche dello sviluppo embrionale dei Selaci. 1, 2, 3. *Pubbl. Stazione Zoologica di Napoli*, 12–13.

RIBOT CARBALLAL, C., R. FELIX URAGA, & F. GALVAN MAGAÑA (2003): Age and growth of the shortfin mako, *Isurus oxyrinchus*, from Baja California Sur, Mexico. *AES Abstracts Manaus, Brazil, June 27–June 30*: 6.

ROEDEL, P.M. & W.E. RIPLEY (1950): California sharks and rays. *Fishery Bulletin*, (75): 1–88.

SAMPSON, M. (2008): *Modern Sharking*. Geared Up Publications, 264 pp.

SCIARROTTA, T.C. & D.R. NELSON (1977): Diel behavior of the blue shark, *Prionace glauca*, near Santa Catalina Island, California. *Fishery Bulletin*, 75(3): 519–528.

SHESTOPAL, I.P., O.V. SMIRNOV, & A.A. GREKOV (2002): Bottom long-line fishing for deepwater sharks on sea-mounts in the International waters of the North Atlantic. *NAFO SCR Doc. 02/100*, Ser. No. N4721, 5 pp.

SICCARDI, E.M. (1971): *Cetorhinus* in el Atlantico sur (Elasmobranchii: Cetorhinidae). *Revista del Museo Argentino de Ciencias Naturales "Bernardino Rivadavia"*, 6(2): 61–101.

SIMS, D.W. & V.A. QUAYLE (1998): Selective foraging behaviour of basking sharks on zooplankton in a small-scale front. *Nature*, 393: 460–464.

SKOMAL, G.B. & L.J. NATANSON (2002): Age and growth of the blue shark, *Prionace glauca*, in the North Atlantic Ocean. *Col. Vol. Sci. Pap. ICCAT*, 54(4): 1212–1230.

SKOMAL, G. B., G. WOOD, & N. CALOYIANI (2004): Archival tagging of a basking shark, *Cetorhinus maximus*, in the western North Atlantic. *Journal of the Marine Biological Association of the UK*, 84: 795–799.

SKOMAL, G. B., S.I. ZEEMAN, J.H. CHISHOLM, E.L. SUMMERS, H.J. WALSH, K.W. MCMAHON, & S.R. THORROLD (2009): Transequatorial Migrations by Basking Sharks in the Western Atlantic Ocean. *Current Biology*, 19(1–4).

SMALE, M.J. & P.C. HEEMSTRA (1997): First record of albinism in the great white shark, *Carcharodon carcharias* (Linnaeus, 1758). *South African Journal of Science*, 93: 243–245.

STEVENS, J.D. (ed.) (1987): *Sharks.* Intercontinental Publishing Corporation Limited, Hong Kong, 240 pp.

STILLWELL, C. (1991): The ravenous mako. Pp. 77–88 in Gruber, S.H. (ed.) Discovering sharks. *Underwater Naturalist, Bulletin American Littoral Society*, 19(4)–20(1).

STILLWELL, C.E. & N.E. KOHLER (1993): Food habits of the sandbar shark, *Carcharhinus plumbeus*, off the U.S. northeast coast, with estimates of daily ration. *Fishery Bulletin*, 91: 138–150.

STRONG, W.R. Jr. (1996): Shape discrimination and visual predatory tactics in white sharks. Pp. 229–240 in: Klimley, A.P. & D.G. Ainley (eds.): *Great White Sharks. The Biology of* Carcharodon carcharias. Academic Press, San Diego, 518 pp.

TALLACK, S.M.L. & J.W. MANDELMAN (2009): Do rare earth metals deter spiny dogfish? A feasibility study on the use of misch metal to reduce the bycatch of *Squalus acanthias* by hook gear in the Gulf of Maine (USA). *ICES Journal of Marine Science*, 66: 315–322.

TALLACK, S.M.L., L. SLIFKA, & S. WHITFORD (2007): *Industry-science partnership investigating the short-term and long-term discard mortality of spiny dogfish using commercial hook gear in the Gulf of Maine.* Final Report submitted to the Northeast Consortium, 31st July 2007, Gulf of Maine Research Institute (Portland, Maine) and the Cape Cod Commercial Hook Fishermen's Association (Chatham, Massachusetts): 56 pp.

TORTONESE, E. (1956): *Fauna d'Italia vol.II. Leptocardia, Ciclostomata, Selachii.* Calderini, Bologna, 334 pp.

TRICAS, T.C. & J.E. McCOSKER (1984): Predatory behavior of the white shark, *Carcharodon carcharias*, with notes on its biology. *Proceedings of the California Academy of Sciences*, 43(14): 221–238.

UCHIDA, S., M. TODA, K. TESHIMA, & K. YANO (1996): Pregnant white sharks and full-term embryos from Japan. Pp. 139–155 in: Klimley, A.P. & D.G. Ainley (eds.) *Great White Sharks: The Biology of* Carcharodon carcharias. Academic Press, San Diego, 518 pp.

VAN DEINSE, A.B. & M.J. ADRIANI (1953): On the absence of gill rakers in specimens of the basking shark, *Cetorhinus maximus* (Gunner). *Zoologische Mededelingen*, 31(27): 307–310.

VANNUCCINI, S. (1999): Shark utilization, marketing and trade. *FAO Fisheries Technical Paper*, 389: 1–470.

WATTS, S. (2001): *The End of the Line?* WildAid, San Francisco, 62 pp.

WHITEHEAD, P.J.P., M.-L. BAUCHOT, J.C. HUREAU, J. NIELSEN, & E. TORTONESE (eds.) (1984): *Fishes of the North-Eastern Atlantic and the Mediterranean.* Vol. 1. Unesco, Paris.

WILSON, S.G. (2004): Basking sharks, *Cetorhinus maximus*, schooling in the southern Gulf of Maine. *Fisheries Oceanography*, 13: 4, 283–286.

ACKNOWLEDGEMENTS

Many people have contributed to this book. We must pay special homage to Beverly Heim (San Diego, California), who took the time to read and edit the entire manuscript.

Many thanks to Sarah Taylor (New England Aquarium, Boston, Massachusetts, U.S.A.) for taking her precious time to shoot stunning photographs for this book.

We thank the following people for freely sharing their observations and for their assistance in assembling useful material for this book:

Harald Bänsch (SharkProject, Munich, Germany),

Larry Bell (Museum of Science, Boston, Massachusetts),

Tracie Bennitt (Triebold Paleontology, Inc., Woodland Park, Colorado),

Thom Benson (Tennessee Aquarium, Chattanooga, Tennessee),

Karyl K. Brewster-Geisz (National Marine Fisheries Service, Highly Migratory Species Management Division, Silver Spring, Maryland),

Emily Bryant (NOAA Fisheries Service Northeast Regional Office, Gloucester, Massachusetts),

Pedro Miguel Niny Cambraia Duarte (Lisboa, Portugal), Robert L. Cantrell (Alexandria, Virginia),

Cheri F. Collins (Connecticut Archaeology Center, Connecticut State Museum of Natural History, Storrs, Connecticut),

Andrey Dolgov (Polar Research Institute of Marine Fisheries and Oceanography—PINRO— Murmansk, Russia),

Charlie Donilon (SnappaCharters, Wakefield, Rhode Island),

Giuliano Doria (Museo civico di Storia Naturale "G. Doria," Genova, Italia),

William B. Driggers III (National Oceanic and Atmospheric Administration, National Marine Fisheries Service, Pascagoula, Mississippi),

Embedded Exhibitions, LLC (Woodland Park, Colorado),

Bill Fisher (333 Productions, Rhode Island),

Vittorio Gabriotti (Italian Ichthyological Society, Brescia, Italy),

Jeffrey Gallant (Greenland Shark and Elasmobranch Education & Research Group, Drummondville, Québec, Canada),

Alberto Gallucci (Milan, Italy),

Jayne M. Gardiner (Department of Biology, University of South Florida, Tampa, Florida), Mark Harris (Florida Fisheries Consultants, Tampa, Florida),

Karsten E. Hartel (Museum of Comparative Zoology, Harvard University, Cambridge, Massachusetts),

Walter Heim (San Diego, California),

Jessica Heim (San Diego, California),

Aaron Henderson (Department of Marine Science and Fisheries, Sultan Qaboos University, Al-Khod, Oman),

Susan Hochgraf (Biological Research Collections, University of Connecticut, Storrs, Connecticut),

Samuel Paco Iglésias (Station de Biologie Marine de Concarneau, Muséum national d'Histoire naturelle, Concarneau, France),

Carolyn Kirdahy (Museum of Science, Boston, Massachusetts),

Nancy E. Kohler (Apex Predators Program, NOAA/National Marine Fisheries Service, Narragansett, Rhode Island, U.S.A.),

Marie Levine (Global Shark Attack File, Princeton, New Jersey),

Kyle Luckenbill (Academy of Natural Sciences, Philadelphia),

John G. Lundberg (Department of Ichthyology, Academy of Natural Sciences, Philadelphia, Pennsylvania),

Ed Lyman (Massachusetts Division of Marine Fisheries, Vineyard Haven, Massachusetts),

Maryland Coast Dispatch (Berlin, Maryland),

Charlotte J. Mehrtens (Perkins Geology Museum, University of Vermont, Burlington, Vermont),

Northeast Fisheries Science Center (Woods Hole, Massachusetts),

Claudio Perotti (Italian Ichthyological Society, Brescia, Italy),

Antonella Preti (National Marine Fisheries Service, Southwest Fisheries Science Center, La Jolla, California),

Joe Romeiro (333 Productions, Rhode Island),

Mark Sampson (Fish Finder Adventures, Ocean City, Maryland),

Pasquale Scida (NOAA Fisheries Service Northeast Regional Office, Gloucester, Massachusetts),

Greg Sears (Mass Bay Guides, Greenbush, Massachusetts), Sarah Sharp (Marine Mammal Rescue, International Fund for Animal Welfare—IFAW—Yarmouthport, Massachusetts),

Dave Sigworth (The Maritime Aquarium at Norwalk, Connecticut),

Gregory Skomal (Massachusetts Division of Marine Fisheries, Vineyard Haven, Massachusetts),

Rudy Socha (Zoo and Aquarium Visitor, Lorain, Ohio),

Todd Stailey (Tennessee Aquarium, Chattanooga, Tennessee),

Nils E. Stolpe (Garden State Seafood Association, Trenton, New Jersey),

Shelly M.L. Tallack (Gulf of Maine Research Institute, Portland, Maine),

Russell Tayler (www.pawtuxetcove.com, Mobile, Alabama),

Skip Theberge (NOAA Central Library, Silver Spring, Maryland),

Triebold Paleontology, Inc. (Woodland Park, Colorado),

Peter L. Tyack (Marine Mammal Behavior Laboratory, Woods Hole Oceanographic Institution, Woods Hole, Massachusetts),

J. Evan Ward (Department of Marine Sciences, University of Connecticut, Groton, Connecticut),

Gregory J. Watkins-Colwell (Division of Vertebrate Zoology, Yale Peabody Museum of Natural History, New Haven, Connecticut),

Catherine Weisel (Museum of Comparative Zoology, Harvard University, Cambridge, Massachusetts),

Bradley M. Wetherbee (Department of Biological Sciences, University of Rhode Island, Kingston, Rhode Island),

Andrew Williston (Museum of Comparative Zoology, Harvard University, Cambridge, Massachusetts),

Dave Wilson Jr. (Maryland Coastal Bays Program, Ocean City, Maryland),

Sabine Wintner (Natal Sharks Board, Umhlanga Rocks, South Africa),

Kristof Zyskowski (Division of Vertebrate Zoology, Yale Peabody Museum of Natural History, New Haven, Connecticut).

For their help, support, and friendship, our sincere gratitude goes to Alessandra Baldi, Antonio De Maddalena, Pinuccia De Maddalena, Emilio De Maddalena, Eleonora De Maddalena, Elisabetta De Maddalena, Isabella De Maddalena, Sauro Baldi, the students of the BCM school, Francesco Guerrazzi, Gaspare Schillaci, Gianluca Cugini, Gianfranco Della Rovere, Vittorio Gabriotti, Marco Zuffa, Matteo Messa, Michele Masera, Antonella Preti, Ralph S. Collier, Sean R. Van Sommeran, Brian May, Paul Rodgers, the Mediterranean Shark Research Group, and the Italian Ichthyological Society.

Our gratitude also goes to our publisher, without whom this book would not be possible, with special thanks to our editor, Michael Steere, for his tireless kindness.

Finally, very special thanks to Richard Ellis for providing the Foreword.

INDEX

Basking shark. (Chris Gotschalk)